Gayle Allen

None of Us Will Return

Charlotte Delbo

NONE OF US WILL RETURN

Translated by John Githens

BEACON PRESS *BOSTON*

Beacon Press books are published under the auspices
of the Unitarian Universalist Association
Published simultaneously in Canada by
Fitzhenry & Whiteside Ltd., Toronto

(paperback)   9   8   7   6   5   4   3   2   1

Library of Congress Cataloging in Publication Data

Delbo, Charlotte.
    None of us will return.
    Translation of Aucun de nous ne reviendra.
    Reprint of the 1968 ed. published by Grove Press,
New York.
    1. Oswięcim (Concentration camp). 2. Delbo,
Charlotte. 3. World War, 1939–1945—Personal
narratives, French. 4. Prisoners of war—Germany—
Biography. I. Title.
[D805.P7D413 1978]   940.54′72′43094385   77–88586
ISBN 0-8070-6371-1

STREET FOR ARRIVALS, STREET FOR DEPARTURES

There are people arriving. They scan the crowd of those who wait seeking those who wait for them. They kiss them and they say that they are tired from the journey.

There are people leaving. They say good-by to those who are not leaving and they kiss the children.

There is a street for people arriving and a street for people leaving.

There is a café called "Arrivals" and a café called "Departures."

There are people arriving and there are people leaving.

But there is a station where those arriving are the same as those leaving

a station at which those arriving have never arrived, to which those leaving have never returned

it is the biggest station in the world.

This is the station at which they arrive, wherever they come from.

They arrive here after days and nights

after crossing whole countries

they arrive here with children, even babies, who were not supposed to have been taken

They have brought their children because you do not part with children for this journey.

Those who had gold brought it along because they thought that gold might be useful.

Everyone brought his dearest possession because you must not leave what is dear to you when you go far away.

Everyone has brought his life along, above all it was his life that he had to bring along.

And when they arrive
they think they have arrived
in Hell
possibly. Still they did not believe it.
They did not know that you could take a train to Hell
but since they are here, they steel themselves and feel ready
to face it
with women, children, aged parents
with family keepsakes and family documents.

They do not know that you do not arrive at that station.
They expect the worst—they do not expect the unthinkable.
And when the soldiers shout to them to line up by fives,
men on one side, women and children on the other, in a
language they do not understand, they understand the blows
of the truncheons and line up by fives since they are ready
for anything.
Mothers clutch their children—they shudder at the thought
that the children might be taken away from them—because
the children are hungry and thirsty and crumpled from not
having slept across so many lands. At long last they are
arriving, they will be able to take care of them.
And when the soldiers shout to them to leave bundles and
blankets and keepsakes on the platform they leave them because they ought to be ready for anything and do not wish
to be surprised at anything. They say "We'll see"; they have
already seen so much and they are tired from the journey.

The station is not a station. It is the end of a line. They
look and they are stricken by the desolation about them.
In the morning, fog hides the marshes.
In the evening, spotlights illuminate the white barbed-wire
fences with the sharpness of stellar photography. They be-

lieve that this is where they are being taken, and they are terrified.

At night, they wait for daylight with the children weighing down their mothers' arms. Wait and wonder.

In the daytime they do not wait. The lines start moving right away. Women and children first, they are the most weary. The men next. They are also weary but relieved that wives and children are being taken care of first.

For the women and children always go first.

In the winter they are gripped by the cold. Especially those who come from Crete. Snow is new to them.

In the summer the sun blinds them as they step down from the dark boxcars that were sealed shut at the start of the journey.

At the start of the journey from France from the Ukraine from Albania from Belgium from Slovakia from Italy from Hungary from the Peloponnesus from Holland from Macedonia from Austria from Herzegovina from the shores of the Black Sea from the shores of the Baltic from the shores of the Mediterranean and from the banks of the Vistula.

They would like to know where they are. They do not know that this is the center of Europe. They look for the name of the station. It is a station without a name.

A station which for them will never have a name.

There are some who are traveling for the first time in their lives.

There are some who have traveled to every part of the globe, businessmen. All landscapes were familiar to them but they do not recognize this one.

They look. Later on they will be able to tell how it was.

Everyone wants to recall what his impression was and how he had the feeling that he would never return.

It is a feeling one might have had already in one's life. They know feelings should not be trusted.

There are those who come from Warsaw with big shawls and knotted bundles
those who come from Zagreb, women with kerchiefs on their heads
those who come from the Danube with garments knitted by the hearth in multicolored yarns
those who come from Greece, bringing black olives and Turkish Delight
those who come from Monte Carlo
they were in the casino
they are in white tie with shirt fronts that the journey has completely ruined
pot-bellied and bald
they are bankers who played at banking
newlyweds who were leaving the synagogue with the bride dressed in white, wearing a veil, all wrinkled from lying on the floor of the boxcar
the bridegroom dressed in black and top hat with soiled gloves
the relatives and guests, women with beaded bags
who all regret that they were not able to stop off at their homes and change into something less fragile.
The rabbi holds his head up high and walks first. He has always set an example for the others.
There are little girls from boarding school with their identical pleated skirts and their hats with blue streamers. They pull up their stockings carefully as they alight. They walk demurely five by five as though on a Thursday outing, holding one another by the hand and not knowing. What can

8

they do to little girls from boarding school who are with their teacher. The teacher tells them: "Be good, children." They have no wish not to be good.

There are old people who have had news from their children in America. Their knowledge of foreign lands came from postcards. Nothing looked like what they see here. Their children will never believe it.

There are intellectuals. Doctors or architects, composers or poets, recognizable by their walk, by their glasses. They too have seen a great deal in their lifetimes. They have studied a lot. Some have even imagined a great deal in order to write books and nothing they have ever imagined resembles what they see here.

There are all the furriers of the big cities and all the gentlemen's and ladies' tailors all the clothiers who had emigrated to the West and who do not recognize in this place the land of their forebears.

There are the inexhaustible multitudes of the cities where each man occupies his own pigeonhole and now in this place they form endless lines and you wonder how all that could fit into the stacked pigeonholes of the cities.

There is a mother who slaps her five-year-old because he does not want to give her his hand and because she wants him to keep still at her side. You run the risk of getting lost you must not become separated in a strange place in such a crowd. She slaps her child and we who know do not forgive her for it. Besides it would make no difference if she were to smother him with kisses.

There are those who journeyed eighteen days who went mad and killed one another in the boxcars and
those who had been suffocated during the journey because they had been packed in so tightly
of course they do not get off.

There is a little girl who hugs her doll to her heart, you can smother dolls too.

There are two sisters in white coats who went out for a walk and did not return for dinner. Their parents are still worrying.

In ranks of five they move along the street for arrivals. They do not know it is the street for departures. You only pass this way once.

They move in strict order—so that you cannot fault them for anything.

They come to a building and they sigh. At last they have arrived.

And when the soldiers shout to the women to strip they undress the children first taking care not to wake them up completely. After days and nights of travel they are fretful and cross

and they begin to get undressed in front of their children, it can't be helped

and when the soldiers hand each one of them a towel they worry if the water in the shower will be warm because the children might catch cold

and when the men come in to the shower room through another door naked too the women hide their children against their bodies.

And then perhaps they understand.

And it is useless for them to understand now since they cannot tell those who are waiting on the platform

cannot tell those who are riding in the dark boxcars across all the countries on the way here

cannot tell those who are in detention camps and are apprehensive about their departure because they fear the climate or the work and because they are afraid of leaving their belongings

cannot tell those who are in hiding in the mountains and in the woods and who no longer have the patience to stay in hiding. Come what may they will return to their homes. Why would they be taken away from their homes they have never done any harm to anyone

cannot tell those who did not want to go into hiding because you cannot go and leave everything

cannot tell those who thought they had put their children in a safe place in a Catholic boarding school where the sisters are so kind.

A band will be dressed in the little girls' pleated skirts. The commandant wants Viennese waltzes on Sunday mornings.

A blockhova,* to give her window a homey touch, will make curtains out of the holy cloth the rabbi wore so that he would be ready to perform services no matter what happened wherever he might be.

A kapo† will dress up in the morning coat and top hat and her girlfriend in the veil and they will play bride and groom at night when the others have collapsed in their bunks from exhaustion. The kapos can have a good time they are not tired in the evening.

Black olives and Turkish Delight will be distributed to the German women prisoners who are sick but they do not like Calamata olives nor olives in general.

And all day and all night

every day and every night the chimneys smoke with this

*A prisoner who is the head of a block.—*Trans.*
†A prisoner who is the foreman of labor detail, responsible to the detail leader.—*Trans.*

fuel from all the countries of Europe

men assigned to the chimneys spend their days sifting the ashes to recover melted gold from gold teeth. They all have gold in their mouths these Jews and they are so many that it makes tons.

And in the spring men and women spread the ashes on the marshes drained and plowed for the first time and fertilize the soil with human phosphate.

They have bags tied to their bellies and they stick their hands into the human bone meal which they scatter by the handful over the furrows with the wind blowing the dust back into their faces and in the evening they are all white with lines traced by the sweat that has trickled down over the dust.

And no fear of running short train after train arrives they arrive every day every night every hour of every day and every hour of every night.

It is the biggest railway station in the world for arrivals and departures.

It is only those who go into the camp who find out what has happened to the others and who weep at having left them at the station because that day the officer ordered the younger people to form a separate line

there has to be someone to drain the marshes and to scatter the ashes of the others

and they say to themselves that it would have been better never to have entered and never to have found out.

You who have wept for two thousand years
for one who suffered three days and three nights

what tears will you have
for those who suffered
many more than three hundred nights and many more than
    three hundred days
how much
will you weep
for those who suffered so many agonies
and they were countless

They did not believe in resurrection to eternal life
And they knew that you would not weep.

O you who know
did you know that hunger makes the eyes sparkle
    that thirst dims them
O you who know
did you know that one can see one's mother dead
    and not cry
O you who know
did you know that in the morning one wants to die
    that in the evening one is afraid
O you who know
did you know that one day is more than a year
    one minute more than a lifetime
O you who know
did you know that legs are more vulnerable than eyes
    nerves harder than bones
    the heart firmer than steel
Did you know that the stones of the road do not weep
    that there is only one word for terror
    only one word for anguish
Did you know that suffering has no limit
    horror no boundary
    Did you know it
You who know.

My mother
she was hands
she was a face
They set our mothers before us naked

Here mothers are no longer mothers to their children.

All were marked on the arm with an indelible number
All were to die naked

Tattooing identified the dead men and women.

It was a desolate plain
at the edge of a town

The plain was icy
and the town
had no name.

DIALOGUE "You are French?"

"Yes."

"So am I."

She has no F on her chest. A star.

"Where are you from?"

"Paris."

"Have you been here long?"

"Five weeks."

"I've been here sixteen days."

"That's already a long time, I know."

"Five weeks. . . . How is it possible?"

"You see . . ."

"And you think we can last it out."

She begs.

"We must try."

"You, you can hope but we . . ."

She points to my striped jacket and she points to her coat, much too big, much too dirty, much too tattered.

"Oh, our chances are the same, you know."

"There's no hope for us."

And her hand makes a gesture and the gesture evokes rising smoke.

"We must fight with all our strength."

"Why. . . . Why fight since all of us have to . . ."

The hand completes the gesture. Rising smoke.

"No. We must fight."

"How can we hope to get out of here. How could anyone ever get out of here. It would be better to throw ourselves on the barbed wire right now."

What is there to say to her. She is small, sickly. And I am unable to persuade myself. All arguments are senseless. I am at odds with my reason. One is at odds with all reason.

18

The chimney smokes. The sky is low. Smoke trails over the camp and billows downward and engulfs us in smells of burning flesh.

THE DUMMIES "Look. Look."

We were crouched on our tier, on the boards that were at the same time bed, table, floor. The ceiling was very low. We just fit if we sat down with our heads bent forward. There were eight of us, our group of eight friends whom death would separate, on this narrow platform that served us as a perch. Soup had been passed out. We had waited outdoors for a long time to file past the soup kettle that steamed into the face of the stubhova.* With her right sleeve rolled up, she plunged the ladle into the kettle in order to dish up the soup. She yelled from behind the steam rising from the soup. The steam muffled her voice. She yelled because there was shoving and talking. We waited sullenly, our hands numb from holding our mess tins. Now with our soup in our laps, we ate. The soup was dirty, but it tasted hot.

"Look, did you see in the yard . . ."

"Oh!" Yvonne P. drops her spoon. She is no longer hungry.

The barred window looks out on the yard of block 25, a yard enclosed by walls. There is a gate that opens into the camp, but if the gate swings open when you are passing by, you run as fast as you can, you do not try to see the gate nor what may lie beyond. You flee. We have a window, we can see. We never turn our heads in that direction.

"Look. Look."

At first we are not sure of what we see. It is difficult at first to distinguish them from the snow. The yard is full of them. Naked. Lying close to each other on the snow. White, a white that looks bluish against the snow. Their heads are shaven, their pubic hairs are straight and stiff. The corpses are frozen. White with brown nails. Their upturned toes are truly ridiculous. Terrible, ridiculous.

*A woman prisoner in charge of a section of a block, under the blockhova.

Boulevard de Courtais in Montluçon. I was waiting for my father at the department store. It was summer, the sun was hot on the asphalt. A truck had stopped and some men were unloading it. It was a shipment of dummies for the store window. Each man picked up a dummy in his arms and set it down at the entrance to the store. The dummies were naked, with conspicuous joints. The men carried them carefully and laid them near the wall on the hot sidewalk.

I watched. I was disturbed by the nakedness of the dummies. I had often seen dummies in the window with their dresses, their shoes and their wigs, their arms set in affected gestures. I had never dreamed that they might be naked, without hair. I had never dreamed that they might be naked outside the display window, away from electric light, and their gestures. Discovering this had the same effect on me as seeing a dead body for the first time.

Now the dummies are lying in the snow, bathed in a winter light that makes me remember the sunlight on the asphalt.

The women who are lying there in the snow are our companions of yesterday. Yesterday they were on their feet at roll call. They stood in rows of five on either side of the Lagerstrasse. They went off to work, they trudged toward the marshes. Yesterday they were hungry. They had lice, they scratched themselves. Yesterday they gulped down the dirty soup. Yesterday they had diarrhea and they were beaten. Yesterday they suffered. Yesterday they longed to die.

Now they are over there, naked corpses in the snow. They are dead in block 25. Death in block 25 does not have the serenity one expects of it, even here.

One morning, because they were fainting at roll call, because they were more ashen than the others, an SS beckoned to them. He formed them into a column which magnified all the additional individual weaknesses that had hitherto been hidden in the mass. And the column, under the command of the SS, was driven toward block 25.

There were women who had gone there alone. Voluntarily. As if to commit suicide. They waited for an SS to go inside for an inspection so that the gate might swing open and they might go in.

There were also women who did not run fast enough one day when we had to run.

There were also women whose comrades had been forced to leave them at the gate, and who had cried: "Don't leave me. Don't leave me."

They had been hungry and thirsty for days, thirsty especially. They had been cold, sleeping practically without clothing on boards, without straw or blankets. Shut in with the dying or the mad, they awaited their turn to die or to go mad. In the morning they went out. They were driven out with blows from a cudgel. Blows from a cudgel for the dying and the mad. The living had to drag the nightly dead out into the yard, because the dead had to be counted too. The SS would pass by. He enjoyed setting his dog on them. Shrieks were heard throughout the whole camp. These were the shrieks of night. Then silence. The roll call was over. This was the silence of day. The living went back in. The dead remained in the snow. They had been stripped. Their clothing would do for others.

Every second or third day trucks came to get the living to take them to the gas chambers, to get the dead and dump them into the crematory ovens. Madness must have been the last refuge of the women who entered there. Some whose tenacious hold on life made them shrewd escaped at the outset. Sometimes they lingered on for a few weeks, never more than three, in block 25. We would see them at the bars of the windows. They would beg: "Something to drink. Something to drink." There are talking ghosts.

"Look. Oh! I tell you she moved. That one, the next to the last. Her hand . . . her fingers are opening, I'm sure of it."

The fingers open slowly, the snow blossoms into a discolored sea anemone.

"Don't look. Why do you look?" pleads Yvonne P., her eyes wide, riveted to a corpse that is still alive. "Eat your soup," says Cecile. "They have no need of anything now."

I look too. I watch this corpse that moves and to which I am insensitive. I am a grown woman now. I can look at naked dummies without being afraid.

THE MEN

In the morning and in the evening, on the road to the marshes, we met columns of men. Jews were in civilian clothes. Worn-out clothes with a cross in red lead paint smeared on the back. Shapeless garments that they fastened about themselves. The others were in stripes. The uniforms flapped on their skinny backs.

We pitied them because they had to march in step. We walked as best we could. The kapo at the head was fat and well shod, warmly dressed. He called time: "Links, zwei, drei, vier. Links." The men had trouble following. They were wearing canvas slippers with wooden soles that did not stay on their feet. We wondered how they could march with those slippers. When there was snow or ice they carried them in their hands.

They had the gait we all had. Head thrust forward, neck thrust forward. Head and neck drag the rest of the body along. Head and neck pull the feet. In their gaunt faces, their eyes burned, dark-circled, black. Their lips were swollen, black or too red, and when they parted them bleeding gums showed.

They passed near us. We murmured "French, French" to find out if there were any of our fellow countrymen among them. So far we had not met any.

All intent on marching, they did not look at us. We looked at them. We looked at them and wrung our hands in pity. The thought of them pursued us, and their gait, and their eyes.

There were so many sick people among us who did not eat that we had lots of bread. We tried everything to get them to eat, to overcome the disgust that the food aroused in them, to eat so as to survive. Our arguments did not rouse their wills. From the moment of arrival, they had given up.

24

One morning we took some bread out under our jackets. For the men. We meet no column of men. We wait impatiently for evening. On our way back we hear their tread behind us. Drei. Vier. Links. They march faster than we do. We must move aside to let them pass. Poles? Russians? Pitiable men, bleeding from misery like all the men here.

When they overtake us we quickly take out our bread and toss it to them. Instantly there is a scramble. They catch the bread, they fight over it, they snatch it from one another. They have the eyes of wolves. Two men roll over into a ditch after a piece that eludes their grasp.

We watch them fight and we weep.

The SS screams and sets his dog on them. The column regroups, resumes the march. Links, zwei, drei.

They did not turn their heads in our direction.

ROLL CALL The SS in black cloaks have passed. They have counted. We wait some more.

We wait.

For days, the next day.

Since the day before, the morrow.

Since the middle of the night, today.

We wait.

Day is breaking.

We wait for day because we must wait for something.

We do not wait for death. It waits for us.

We do not wait for anything.

We wait for what happens. Night because it follows day. Day because it follows night.

We wait for the end of the roll call.

The end of the roll call is the blast of a whistle that makes each woman turn around toward the gate. Motionless ranks become ranks ready to begin the march. The march to the marshes, to the bricks, to the ditches.

Today we wait longer than usual. The sky is paler than usual. We wait.

What?

An SS appears at the end of the Lagerstrasse, comes toward us, stops in front of our ranks. By the caduceus on his cap he must be the doctor. He looks us over. Slowly. He speaks. He does not scream. He speaks. A question. No one answers. He calls: "Interpreter." Marie-Claude comes forward. The SS repeats his question and Marie-Claude translates: "He is asking if there are any among us who cannot endure the roll call." The SS watches us. Magda, our blokhova, who is standing next to him, watches us and moving a bit to the side blinks slightly.

Who in fact can endure the roll call? Who can stand

26

motionless for hours? In the middle of night. In the snow. Without having eaten, without having slept. Who can withstand this cold for hours?

Some raise their hands.

The SS has them step out of the ranks. Counts them. Too few. Softly he utters another sentence and Marie-Claude translates again: "He is asking whether there aren't any others, elderly or sick, who find the roll call too hard in the morning." Other hands go up. Then Magda quickly nudges Marie-Claude and Marie-Claude, without changing her tone: "But it is better not to say so." The hands that have been raised are lowered. All but one. A little old woman, quite tiny, who raises herself up on tiptoe, stretching and waving her arm as high as she can, afraid that they will not see her. The SS moves on. The old woman speaks up: "I, Sir, I am sixty-seven years old." Her neighbors shush her. She gets angry. Why would they stop her if there is a less harsh routine for the sick and the aged, why would they stop her from taking advantage of this? In despair at having been forgotten, she cries out. In a shrill voice as aged as herself, she cries out: "Me, Sir. I'm sixty-seven years old." The SS hears, turns around: "Komm," and she joins the group just now formed, which the SS doctor escorts to block 25.

Magda had been in the camp for a year.

She knew.

ONE DAY She clung to the slope, clung with her hands and her feet to the snow-covered slope. Her whole body was tensed, her jaws were tensed, her neck with its wrenched cartilage was tensed, all that remained of muscle on her bones was tensed.

And her efforts were futile—the efforts of a person pulling an imaginary rope.

She was arched from her forefinger to her great toe but each time she reached out her hand to grip higher and try to climb the slope, she fell back. Her body would suddenly become flaccid, pitiable. She would then raise her head and one could read on her face the mental strain that was going on within her to reposition her limbs for the push. Her teeth clenched, her chin thrust out. Her ribs protruded like hoops under her tight garment, a civilian coat—a Jewess—her ankles stiffened. She tried again to hoist herself onto another snowbank.

Each of her gestures was so slow and so awkward, so indicative of weakness that one wondered how she could possibly move. At the same time it was difficult to understand why she had to work so hard, in a manner so disproportionate to the enterprise and to a body which could not have weighed anything.

Now her hands clutched a crust of hardened snow, her feet without support sought a rough spot, a toehold. They kicked in thin air. Her legs were wrapped in rags. They were so thin that despite the rags they made one think of the dangling bean poles people put on scarecrows to represent legs. Especially when they kicked in thin air. She slipped back to the bottom of the ditch.

She turns her head as if to measure the distance, looks upward. One can see the confusion mount in her eyes, in her hands, in her contorted face.

"Why do all those women look at me like that? Why are they there and why are they lined up in close ranks and why do they stand there without moving? They look at me and they do not seem to see me. They do not see me, they would not stand there like that. They would help me up. Why don't you help me, you who are so near? Help me. Pull me. Lean over. Stretch out your hand, oh! they are not budging."

And her hand writhed toward us in a desperate appeal. Her hand falls back—a faded mauve star on the snow. Once fallen, it lost its wasted look, it softened, became once again something living and pitiable. The elbow props itself up, slips. The whole body slumps.

In the background, beyond the barbed wire, the plain, the snow, the plain.

We were all there, several thousand of us, standing in the snow since morning—this is what one must call night since morning came at three A.M. Daybreak had lit up the snow which had hitherto lit up the night and the cold had grown more intense.

Standing motionless since the middle of the night, we became so heavy on our legs that we sank into the ground, into the ice, powerless against numbness. The cold bruised our temples, our jawbones, to the point that we thought the bones were dislocated, that our skulls were bursting. We had given up hopping from one foot to another, clicking our heels, rubbing our palms together. These were exhausting exercises.

We stood motionless. The will to struggle and resist, life, had taken refuge in a reduced part of the body, just the immediate vicinity of the heart.

We stood there motionless, several thousand women speaking every language, huddled against one another, bowing our heads under the stinging flurries of snow.

We stood there motionless, reduced to the beating of our hearts alone.

Where is she going, the one who is breaking rank? She moves like a sick person or a blind man, a blind man who looks. She heads toward the ditch with a wooden gait. She is at the edge, crouches to climb down. She falls. Her foot slips on the crumbling snow. Why does she want to go down into the ditch? She broke rank without hesitation, without hiding from the SS who stood stiffly in her black cloak, stiffly in her black boots, guarding us. She went off as if she were somewhere else, on a street where she might cross from one sidewalk to the other, or in a park. Bringing up a park here may make you laugh. Perhaps one of those crazy old women who frighten children in parks. She is a young woman, a girl almost. Such frail shoulders.

Now she is at the bottom of the ditch with her hands clawing and her feet fumbling, lifting the weight of her head with an effort. Now her face is turned toward us. Her cheeks are violet, accentuated, her mouth swollen, very dark purple, her eye sockets deeply shadowed. Her face is the face of naked despair.

For a long while she struggles against the unruliness of her limbs to right herself. She flounders like a drowning man. Then she stretches up her hands to pull herself to the other side. Her hand seeks something to grip, her nails scrape the snow, her whole body stretches convulsively. And she drops back, exhausted.

It is so painful that I do not watch her any more. I do not want to watch her any more. I want to change places, not see her any more. Not see those holes at the back of her eye sockets any more, those holes that stare. What does she want to do? Does she want to reach the electrified fence? Why does she stare at us? Am I not the one whom she is singling out? I the one whom she is beseeching? I turn my head. To look elsewhere. Elsewhere.

Elsewhere—in front of us—the gate of block 25.

Standing, wrapped in a blanket, a child, a little boy. A tiny shaven head, a face in which the jaws and the brow ridge stand out. Barefoot, he jumps up and down without stopping, with a frenzied movement that makes one think of that of savages dancing. He wants to wave his arms too to keep warm. The blanket slips open. It is a woman. A skeleton of a woman. She is naked. One can see her ribs and hip bones. She pulls the blanket up on her shoulders and continues to dance. A mechanical dance. A dancing skeleton of a woman. Her feet are small, thin and bare in the snow. There are living, dancing skeletons.

And now I am sitting in a café writing this story—for this is turning into a story.

The weather clears. Is it afternoon? We have lost track of time. The sky shows through. Very blue. A forgotten blue. Hours have passed since I managed to stop watching the woman in the ditch. Is she still there? She reached the top of the slope—how did she manage that—and she stopped there. Her hands are drawn to the sparkling snow. She takes a handful and brings it to her lips in an exasperatingly slow gesture which must cost her infinite effort. She sucks the snow. We understand why she left the ranks with such resolution in her features. She wanted some clean snow for her swollen lips. Since daybreak she had been fascinated by this clean snow that she wanted to reach. On this side the snow that we have trampled is black. She sucks her snow but she seems to have lost interest in doing so. Snow does not quench thirst when you have a fever. All that effort for a handful of snow which in her mouth is a handful of salt. Her hand drops, her neck bends. A fragile stalk that must break. Her back hunches, her shoulder blades protrude through the thin material of her coat. It is a yellow coat, the color of our dog Flac who grew so thin after his illness and whose whole body grew round like the skeleton of a bird in a museum just before he died. The woman is going to die.

She does not look at us any more. She lies in the snow, her body contorted. His spine arched, Flac is about to die—the first creature I ever saw die. Mama, Flac is at the garden gate. He is all hunched up. He is trembling. André says he is going to die.

"I must get up, must get up. I must walk. I must struggle on. Won't they help me? Help me all you who are standing there doing nothing."

Mama, come quick, Flac is going to die.

"I know why they don't help me. They are dead. They are dead. They seem alive because they are standing propped up against one another. They are dead. I do not want to die."

Her hand waves once again like a cry—and she does not cry out. In what language would she cry if she were to cry out.

A dead woman moves toward her. A dummy in a striped garment. In two steps the dead woman reaches her, pulls her by the arm, drags her up on our side so that she may take her place in the ranks again. The black cloak of the SS has approached. It is nothing more than a dirty yellow sack that the dead woman drags toward us, that refuses to budge. Hours pass. What can we do? She is going to die. Flac, you know our yellow dog who was so thin, is going to die. More hours.

Suddenly a shiver runs through this heap that the yellow coat makes in the slush. The woman is trying to get to her feet. Her actions break down into unbearable slow motion. She kneels, looks at us. None of us move. She leans her hands on the ground—her body is arched and thin like Flac's, who was going to die. She manages to stand up. She totters, seeks something to steady herself. There is nothing. She walks.

She walks in the empty space. She is so bent over that one wonders why she does not fall again. No. She walks. She staggers but she moves on. And the bones of her face display a terrible resolution. We see her cross the empty space in front of our ranks. Where is she going now?

"Why are you surprised that I am walking? Didn't you hear him call me, that one, the SS who is in front of the gate with his dog. You didn't hear because you are dead."

The SS woman in the black cloak has left. Now it is an SS man in green who is in front of the gate.

The woman advances. It is as if she were obeying an order. In front of the SS she stops. Her back is racked with convulsions, her hunched back with the shoulder blades protruding beneath her yellow coat. The SS holds his dog on a leash. Did he give an order, make a sign? The dog pounces on the woman—without growling, without snarling, without barking. It is as silent as a dream. The dog pounces on the woman, sinks its teeth into her throat. And we do not move, stuck in a viscous substance that prevents us from making even a gesture—as in a dream. The woman screams. A wrenched-out scream. A single scream that rends the immobility of the plain. We do not know if the cry comes from her or from us, from her torn throat or from ours. I feel the teeth of the dog at my throat. I scream. I shriek. Not a sound comes out of me. The silence of a dream.

The plain. The snow. The plain.

The woman collapses. A shudder and it is over. Something snaps. The head in the slush is no more than a stump. The eyes make dirty wounds.

"All these dead women who no longer look at me." Mama, Flac is dead. He was a long time dying. Then he dragged himself to the steps. There was a rattle that blocked his throat and he died. It was as if someone had strangled him.

33

The SS tugs on the leash. The dog lets go. He has a bit of blood on his muzzle. The SS whistles, goes away.

Before the gate of block 25 the blanket with the bare feet and the shaven head has not stopped jumping up and down. Night is coming on.

And we remain standing in the snow. Motionless in the motionless plain.

And now I am in a café writing this.

MARIE Her father, her mother, her brothers and her sisters were gassed on arrival.

Her parents were too old, the children too young. She says: "My little sister was beautiful.

You cannot imagine how beautiful she was.

They must not have looked at her.

If they had looked at her, they would not have killed her.

They would not have been able to."

THE NEXT DAY The roll call began when it was night and now it is day. The night was clear and cold, crackling with frost—that trickle of ice that runs down from the stars. The day is clear and cold, almost unbearably clear and cold. A whistle. The columns move. The movement works its way down to us. Unconsciously, we have faced about. Unconsciously, we move too. We advance. So numb that we seem to be only a chunk of cold that advances in one piece. Our legs move on as if they were not a part of us. The first columns pass through the gate. On either side SS with their dogs. They are bundled in their cloaks, their woolen helmets, their mufflers. The dogs too, in their dog blankets, with the two black letters SS on a white circle. Blankets made from flags. The columns stretch out. We have to dress ranks to pass through the gate, to space ourselves. Once past the gate we huddle together like animals but the cold is so intense that we no longer feel it. Before us sparkles the plain: the sea. We follow. The ranks cross the road, move straight toward the sea. In silence. Slowly. Where are we going? We move onward into the sparkling plain. We move onward into the light solidified by the cold. The SS shout. We do not understand what they shout. The columns strike out into the sea, farther and farther into the icy light. The SS repeat their orders over our heads. We move onward blinded by the snow. And suddenly we are seized with fear, with dizziness at the edge of this blinding plain. What do they want? What are they going to do with us? They shout. They run and their arms jingle. What are they going to do with us?

Then the columns form into squares. Ten ranks of ten. One square after another. A gray checkerboard on the shimmering snow. The last column. The last column comes to a halt. Shouts so that the edges of the checkerboard will become quite sharp on the snow. The SS guard the corners. What do they want to do? An officer on horseback passes. He looks at the perfect squares that fifteen thousand women form on the snow. He wheels around, satisfied. The shouting stops. The sentries begin to walk back and forth around the squares. We become conscious of ourselves again, we are still breathing. We breathe the cold. Beyond us the plain.

The snow sparkles with refracted light. There are no beams, only light, hard and glacial light against which everything is etched in sharp outline. The sky is blue, hard and glacial. One thinks of plants frozen fast in ice. In the Arctic ice must form around underwater plants. We are frozen fast in a hard block of ice as transparent as a block of crystal. And this crystal is bathed in light, as though light were frozen in the ice, as though the ice were light. It takes us a long time to realize that we can budge inside the block of ice. We wriggle our feet inside our shoes, try to stamp our feet. Fifteen thousand women stamp their feet and it makes no noise. The silence is solidified into cold. The light is immobile. We are in a setting in which time is abolished. We do not know if we exist, only ice, light, dazzling snow, and us, in this ice, in this light, in this silence.

We remain motionless. The morning drains away—time outside of time. And the edge of the checkerboard is no longer so sharp. The ranks are coming apart. Some women take a step or two, return to their places. The snow sparkles, immense, over the expanse where nothing casts a shadow. Pared down to sharp lines, the light poles, the roofs of the barracks almost buried in snow, barbed wire drawn in pen and ink. What do they want to do with us?

Time runs on but the light does not change. It remains hard, icy, solid, the sky just as blue, just as hard. The ice draws tighter on our shoulders, it grows heavier, crushes us. Not that we feel colder, we just become more and more inert, more and more unfeeling. We are embedded in a block of crystal beyond which, far off in our memories, we see the living. Viva says: "I will no longer like winter sports." Strange that snow could evoke for her something besides a deadly, hostile, unnatural and hitherto unfamiliar element.

At our feet a woman sits down in the snow, awkwardly. We hold back from saying to her: "Not in the snow, you'll catch cold." It is still a reflex action of the memory and of former notions. She sits in the snow and makes a hole for herself. A recollection of childhood readings, animals that make a bed to die in. The woman works with small and precise gestures, stretches out. Her face in the snow, she groans softly. Her hands open. She is silent.

We watch without comprehending.

The light is still immobile, wounding, cold. It is the light of a dead star. And the vast frozen expanse, infinitely dazzling, is that of a dead planet.

Immobile in the ice in which we are caught fast, inert, unfeeling, we have lost all the senses of life. No one says: "I am hungry. I am thirsty. I am cold." Transported to another world, we are at the same time exposed to the breath of another life, to living death. In ice, in light, in silence.

Suddenly a truck appears on the road that skirts the barbed-wire fence. It rides over the snow. Noiselessly. It is an open truck that must be used for hauling gravel. It is loaded with women. They are standing bareheaded. Little shaven heads like little boys', thin faces, crowded together. The truck moves with all these heads outlined in sharp strokes against the blue of the sky. A silent truck that glides by the barbed-wire fence like a precise ghost. A frieze of faces against the sky.

The women pass near us. They cry out. They cry out and we hear nothing. This cold and dry air would be conductive if we were in an ordinary earthly environment. They cry out to us but no sound reaches us. Their mouths cry out, their outstretched arms cry out, and every bit of them cries out. Each body is a cry. So many torches that flame in cries of terror, so many cries that have assumed the bodies of women. Each woman is a materialized cry, a scream that is not heard. The truck moves silently over the snow, passes under a portico, disappears. It carries off the cries.

Another truck exactly like the first, also loaded with women, who cry out and whom we do not hear, glides past and disappears under the portico. Then a third. This time it is we who cry out, a cry which the ice in which we are frozen fast does not transmit—or are we struck mute? In each truck load, dead women are mingled with the living. The dead are naked, piled up. And the living try hard to avoid touching the dead. But at bumps and jolts they hang on to a rigid arm or leg sticking up over the sides. The living shrink with fear. With fear and revulsion. They shriek. We hear nothing. The truck glides silently over the snow.

We watch with eyes that cry out, that do not believe.

Each face is inscribed with such precision in the icy light, on the blue of the sky, that it is marked there for eternity.

For eternity, shaven heads squeezed together and bursting with cries, mouths twisted with cries that are not heard, hands waving in a mute cry.

The screams remain inscribed on the blue of the sky.

It was the day they emptied block 25. The doomed were loaded into trucks going to the gas chamber. The last of them had to load the corpses to be incinerated before climbing in themselves.

Since the dead were immediately thrown into the crematorium, we wondered:

"Those women in the last truck, the live ones mixed in with the dead, did they go to the gas chamber first, or was the whole load dumped into the ovens?"

They screamed because they knew, but their vocal cords had ruptured in their throats.

And us, we were immured in ice, in light, in silence.

THE SAME DAY We had been turned into statues by the cold, on a pedestal of ice formed by our legs, soldered to the ice on the ground. All gestures had been done away with. Scratching our noses or blowing on our hands was as fantastic a notion as a ghost who would scratch his nose or blow on his hands. Someone says: "I think they are making us go back." But nothing within us replies. We have lost awareness and sensation. We have died to ourselves. "They are making us go back. The first squares are forming ranks." The order reached all the squares. The ranks re-formed by fives. The walls of ice opened out. The first column reached the road.

We leaned on one another to keep from falling. Still we did not feel the strain. Our bodies moved apart from us. Possessed, dispossessed. Abstract. We were unfeeling. We walked with shrunken movements, just what our frozen joints permitted. Without talking. We returned to camp. We had not foreseen a release from the immobility that had lasted since the previous night.

We were returning. The light became less implacable. It was no doubt twilight. Perhaps also because everything was blurred before our eyes, the barbed wire so distinct just a short while before and the sparkling snow now flicked with diarrhea. Dirty puddles. The end of the day. Dead women strewn about on the snow, in the puddles. Sometimes we had to step over them. To us they were everyday obstacles. It was impossible for us to feel anything else. We marched. Automatons marched. Statues of frost marched. Exhausted women marched.

We were going when Josée, in the rank in front, turning toward us says: "When you get to the gate you must run. Pass the word along." She thinks that I do not hear and repeats: "You must run." The order is transmitted without

41

it arousing any wish within us to carry it out, any image of ourselves running. As if someone had said "If it rains, open your umbrella." Just as idiotic.

When a break occurs in the lines in front of us we know that we are at the gate. All start to run. They run. Clogs, poorly fastened shoes fly in all directions but they take no notice of it. They run. In confusion that would be grotesque for a statue of ice, they run. When our turn comes, when we come to the gate, we too break into a run, we run straight ahead, determined without the intervention of our choice or our will to run till we lose our breath. And to us this no longer seems the slightest bit grotesque. We run. Toward what? Why? We run.

I do not know if I understood right away that we had to run—because on either side of the gate and all along the Lagerstrasse, in a double line, stood all that the camp numbered of SS in skirts, of prisoners with armbands or blouses of every color and of every rank, all these were armed with sticks, clubs, straps, belts, and whips, beating and flailing whatever passed between the two rows. To dodge the blows of a club meant to walk smack into the lash of a strap. The blows rained down upon our heads, on the backs of our necks. And the furies screamed: "Schneller! Schneller!" Faster, faster, flailing faster, ever faster this grain that was slipping through, running, running. I do not know if I understood that we had to run because life depended on it. I ran. And it did not occur to anyone to refuse to conform to the absurd. We ran. We ran.

I do not know if I pieced together this whole scene later or if I had an overall conception of it right away on my own. I did have the impression however of having faculties keen and alert to see everything, to grasp everything, to protect myself on all sides. I ran.

It was a mad dash which one would have had to measure from some familiar promontory in order to take full measure of the madness. It was not within the power of any one of us to imagine that she might take an objective viewpoint. We ran. Schneller. Schneller. We ran.

Back inside the camp and out of breath, I hear someone say: "Now to the block. Quick. Go back to the block." The first human voice that one hears upon awakening. I get a good grip on myself and look about me. I had lost my companions. Others swept along after me, recognized one another: "Oh! You're here? And Marie? And Gilberte?"

I come out of the trance whence arose the contorted faces, the apoplectic faces of maddened furies with wild, flying hair. Schneller. Schneller. And that Drexler woman hooking one of the women next to me with the handle of her cane. Who? Who was it? Impossible to remember but all the same I saw her face, her expression frozen by the constriction of her neck from behind. Drexler yanking on her cane, making the woman fall, throwing her to the side. Who was that? Only a spectator would have seen the madness in this rout, for we had yielded at once to the fantastic and we had forgotten the reflexes of the normal human being when confronting the outrageous.

"Go back to the block. Here. This way." The first women to snap to guided the others. I enter the darkness where voices direct me: "This way. There. That's it. Climb up." And I grab hold of the planks to climb up to our platform.

"What were you doing? You were the only one missing and we were beginning to be afraid." Hands hoist me up. "Who were you with?" "With me, we were together," says Yvonne B. She had not left my side, I had not seen her.

"Did you see Hélène?"

"Hélène?"

"Yes, she was on the ground, she gave her arm to Alice Viterbo and both of them fell."

"Alice was caught."

"Hélène tried to pull her along, but Alice couldn't get up again."

"Then Hélène left her."

Hélène was coming. "You managed to get away?"

"Someone pulled me free and dragged me, shouting 'Leave her alone. Leave her alone.' I started to run again. I had to leave Alice behind. Can't someone go and get her?"

"No. We must not leave the block."

One by one the women return. Stunned. Exhausted. Each time, we count ourselves.

"Viva, is all your group there?"

"Yes. All eight."

"Next door, are you all there?"

"No. Madame Brabander is missing."

"Who else is missing?"

"Madame Van der Lee."

"This is Marie."

"And grandma Yvonne?"

We name all the elderly, the sick, the weak.

"I am here," answers the faint voice of grandma Yvonne.

We count again. Fourteen are missing.

I saw Madame Brabander when the Drexler woman stopped her with her cane. She said to her daughter: "Get away. Run. Leave me."

I had run and run without seeing anything. I had run and run without thinking anything, without knowing whether there was danger having only a vague but nearby sensation of it. Schneller. Schneller. Once I had looked at my shoe, the lace was undone, without ceasing to run. I had run without feeling the blows of the clubs, of the belts that struck me.

44

And then I had felt like laughing. Or rather, no, I had seen a double of myself wanting to laugh. My cousin used to tell me that a duck could still walk with its head cut off. And this duck began to run and run, its head fallen behind it, which it did not see, this duck ran like no duck ever ran before, looking at its shoe and not now caring about the rest, with its head cut off it ran no more risks.

We wait, still hoping to see the missing return. They do not come back. It's not as though we were really worried as we waited. It is like second nature to us. And we can explain to ourselves what has happened.

"You understand, they were only letting the young ones through. The ones who ran fast. All the others got caught."

"I wanted so much to drag Alice out. I held her as long as I could."

"Madame Brabander ran very well."

And one sister said to another: "If something like that should happen again, don't bother about me. Save yourself. Just think of yourself. Promise me that, won't you? Swear it."

"Listen, Hélène. With her leg Alice could not have survived under any circumstances."

"They caught lots of Poles too."

"With that wrinkled face, Madame Brabander looked old."

We are already speaking about them in the past tense.

Little Brabander in her bunk has the look of one nothing will touch anymore.

I wonder how a duck can run with its head off. My legs were paralyzed by the cold.

What are they going to do with those women?

The chief of the block, Magda, a Slovak, calls for silence and says something which Marie-Claude translates: "They need some volunteers. It won't take long. The younger

45

women." It seemed impossible to get the slightest possible further effort from our arms, from our legs. For our group, it is Cécile who gets up: "I'll go," and puts her shoes on. "I'd better go and find out what is going on."

When she returned her teeth were chattering, like the sound of castanets. She was frozen. And she was weeping. We rubbed her to warm her up, to stop the shivering that was spreading to us and we questioned her the way one questions a child, with silly words. "It was to pick up the dead that were left in the field. We had to carry them to the front of block 25. There was one who was still alive, she pleaded, she clung to us. We were trying to take her away when someone shouted. 'Run for it! Run for it! Don't stay in front of 25. Taube is coming and he'll throw you in. Run for it!' Our friends are there already, the ones that were caught just now. So we left them and we ran. The dying woman held onto my ankles."

All fourteen died. They said that Antoinette was sent to the gas chamber. Some held on a long time. Apparently Madame Van der Lee went mad. The one who took the longest to die was Alice.

ALICE'S LEG One morning before roll call, little Simone who had gone to the latrines behind block 25 came back all trembling: "Alice's leg is there. Come see."

Behind block 25 was the morgue, a wooden barracks where they piled up the corpses removed from the sick bay. Piled high, they awaited the truck that would bring them to the crematory ovens. The rats devoured them. Through the opening without a door, we could see the heap of naked bodies and the glittering eyes of rats appearing and disappearing. When there were too many bodies, they piled them up outside.

It is a hay rick of corpses as carefully stacked as a real hay rick in the moonlight and the snow, at night. But we look at them without fear. We know that this is the limit of what we can bear and we forbid ourselves to let go.

Lying in the snow, Alice's leg is alive and sentient. It must have detached itself from the dead Alice.

We used to go just to see if it was still there and each time it was intolerable. Alice abandoned, dying in the snow. Alice whom we could not approach because weakness held us rooted to the spot. Alice dying alone and calling no one.

Alice had been dead for weeks while her artificial leg continued to lie on the snow. Then it snowed again. The leg was covered over. It reappeared in the mud. That leg in the mud. Alice's leg—severed alive—in the mud.

We saw it for a long time. One day it was no longer there. Someone must have taken it for firewood. A gypsy woman surely, no one else would have had the courage.

STÉNIA No one can fall asleep tonight.

The wind blows and whistles and moans. The moaning rises from the marshes, a sob that swells and bursts and calms down into a shivery silence, another sob that swells, swells and bursts and dies away.

No one can fall asleep.

And in the silence between the sobbing of the wind, death rattles. Muffled at first, then distinct, then loud, so loud that the ear trying to locate the sounds still hears them when the wind dies down.

Sténia, the blockhova, cannot sleep. She goes out of her room, a small nook at the entry to the block. Her candle tunnels through the dark passage between the tiers on which we are bedded, stacked. Sténia waits until the wind dies down and, in the silence during which troubled breathing is heard, she cries: "Who's making that noise? Quiet!" The death rattles continue. Sténia cries: "Quiet!" and the woman who is dying does not hear. "Quiet!" The rattles fill the silence between the waves of wind, fill all the darkness of the night.

Sténia raises her candle, heads toward the sound, identifies the woman who is dying and orders her to be brought down. Under Sténia's blows, the companions of the dying woman carry her outside. They lay her against the wall, as gently as possible, and go back in to go to bed.

Sténia's light moves off, disappears. Squalls of wind and rain beat down upon the roofing as though to break it.

In the barracks, no one can fall asleep.

A plain
covered with marshes
with hand trucks
with gravel for the hand trucks
with spades and shovels for the marshes
a plain
covered with men and women
the hand trucks and marshes for the spades
a plain
of cold and fever
for men and women
who struggle
in agony
and die.

THE DAY The marshes. The plain covered with marshes. Boundless marshes. The boundless icy plain.

We only pay attention to our feet. Marching in ranks creates a kind of obsession. One continually looks at the feet moving in front. You have these feet that move on, heavily, move on before you, feet that you avoid and that you never overtake, feet that always precede your own, always even at night in a nightmare of tramping, feet that so fascinate you that you would see them even if you were in the first row, feet that shuffle or stumble, that move on. That move on with their irregular noise, their uncoordinated step. And if you are behind someone who is barefoot because her shoes have been stolen, feet that go bare through ice and slush, bare feet—bare in the snow, tortured feet that you wish to see no more, pitiable feet that you are afraid of treading on, that disturb you so much they make you ill. Sometimes a clog leaves a foot, lands in front of you, annoys you like a fly in summer. You do not stop for this clog that someone else bends down to pick up. One has to march. You march. And you pass the straggler cast off from the ranks on the shoulder of the road, who runs to take her place again and can no longer pick out her companions now swallowed up in the mass of others, and who looks back and forth at their feet for she knows she can identify them by their shoes. You march. You march on the road that is as smooth as a skating rink, or sticky with mud. Reddish clay that your soles stick in. You march. You march toward the marshes smothered in the fog. You march without seeing anything, your eyes riveted on the feet that march in front of you. You march. You march into the marsh-covered plain. Marshes all the way to the horizon. Into the endless plain, the frozen plain. You march.

We have been marching since daybreak.

A moment comes when the cold, more humid, more raw, pierces to the bone. The sky grows bright. It is daybreak. They say it is daybreak.

We had waited for daybreak to leave. Every day we waited for daybreak to leave. One could not go out before it got light, before the sentries on the watchtowers could shoot at the runaways. The idea of running away occurred to no one. One has to be strong to want to escape. One has to know that he can count on all his muscles and senses. No one thought of running away.

It was daybreak. The columns formed. We let ourselves be put in any of them. Our only concern was that we should not be separated, so we kept a tight hold on one another.

Once the columns were formed, there was still a long wait. Thousands of women take a long time to come out, five at a time, counted as they pass. Passing through the gate makes us flinch. Passing before the eyes of that Drexler woman, of Taube, before so many scrutinizing eyes that would be drawn to an improperly fastened collar, an open button, hands improperly hanging at our sides, a number not legible enough. In front of the check-point barracks, the SS touched the first woman in each rank with her cane and counted: fünfzehn, zwanzig, up to one hundred, up to two hundred depending on the size of the gang. When this number had passed through, two SS, each holding a dog on a leash, closed the line of march. Coil by coil, the camp disgorged its entrails of the night to the light of day.

We turned either to the right or to the left. To the right toward the marshes. To the left toward the houses to be torn down, the hand trucks to load and to push. For weeks I made the wish that we would turn to the right because then we would pass a brook where I might get water to drink. I had been thirsty for weeks. Most often we went to the marshes.

We started out on the road. The discipline relaxed. We could give one another an arm to help us walk, could pull up our collars, could put our hands in our sleeves. The column stretched out on the road.

Today the road is covered with sheet ice, as smooth as a looking glass. We slide on the ice. We fall. The column marches. There are some whom we must almost carry because they cannot go on, their legs are so swollen. The column marches on. We reach a bend in the road, one that we fear because the wind shifts there. It blows smack in our faces, cutting, icy. The nearness of the marshes can be smelled in the fog. We march in a fog in which nothing can be seen. There is nothing to see. The endless marshes, the plain plunged in fog. The plain wrapped in icy cotton.

We are on the march. Attentive only to our feet, we march. We have been marching since it was barely daybreak.

We march.

When we slow down, the SS who bring up the rear goad their dogs.

We march.

We march into the icy plain.

At the edge of the marsh, the column halts. Each of the forewomen who is in charge of the work counts her detail. Fünfzehn. Zwanzig. Vierzig. Do not move. They are still counting. Dreissig. Fünfzig. Don't move. They recount. Then they lead us to a pile of tools that glint faintly in the fog. We take the spades. To one side there are hand-barrows* piled up. Too bad for those who were not quick enough to get a spade.

Implement in hand, we go down into the marshes. We

---

*Traguet: a hand-barrow, carried by two people, like a stretcher, used for carting bricks stones, etc., in places where a wheelbarrow will not do—such as a marsh.—Trans.

plunge into the denser fog of the marshes. We see nothing in front of us. We slip into the holes, into the ditches. The SS shout. Surefooted in their boots, they come and go and make us run. They mark out the work area. We have to pick up where the spadework had been started the day before. Along a line whose ends are lost in the fog, like so many insects in silhouette, pitiable, defenseless insects, the women take their places, bend over. Everything screams. The SS, the anweiserins, the kapos. We must drive our spades into the ice, attack the ground, lift up the clods, put the clods in the barrow that two women placed next to the furrow hollowed by the spades. When the barrow is loaded, they leave. They walk painfully, their shoulders wrenched by the load. They go to empty the barrow on a mountain of clods that they climb stumbling, falling. The carriers form a continuous belt that tips over, rights itself, bends under the weight, turns the barrow upside down at the top of the heap and comes back to set itself in front of a digger. All along the way clubs on the back of the neck, switches on the temples, straps on the kidneys. Screams. Screams. Screams that scream to the invisible limits of the marsh. It is not insects that are screaming. Insects are mute.

For the diggers, the blows come from behind. There are three furies who come and go, striking everything on their way, never stopping a second, yelling, always yelling the same words, the same insults repeated in that same incomprehensible language, striking one after another, hard, preferably the same ones, the ones they have singled out, one because she is too short and struggles too hard with her spade, another because she is tall and because her height seems defiant to them, still another because her hands are bleeding from frost bite. The SS standing off to the side have made a fire with some sticks. They warm themselves. Their dogs warm themselves too. When the screams reach a peak they join in, scream and strike also. Without knowing. Without reason. With kicks. With punches. Then a hush falls on the marsh as if the mist had thickened and muffled the noise. The screams shatter the silence anew.

This is why we waited for daybreak.

We had waited for daybreak to start the day.

What is nearer to eternity than a day? What is longer than a day? How can one know that it is passing? Clod follows clod, the furrow moves back, the carriers continue their rounds. And screams, screams, screams.

What is longer than a day? Time passes because the fog slowly lifts. Our hands feel less numb. The sun perhaps, distant, hazy. It tears away the tatters of fog bit by bit. The ice softens, softens and melts. Then our feet sink into the mud, our clogs are covered with icy mud right up to our ankles. We stand still in the muddy water, stand still in the icy water. For the barrow carriers the heap of clods becomes more difficult to climb, wet, slippery.

It is day.

The marshes brighten with a hazy, cold radiance as the yellow rays of the sun pierce the mist.

The marsh becomes liquid in the sunshine that has driven the fog away.

It is unmistakably day.

It is day on the marsh where the tall reeds gleam gold.

It is day on the marsh where insects with terror-stricken eyes grow exhausted.

The spade gets heavier and heavier.

The carriers carry their barrows lower and lower.

It is day on the marsh where insects in human form die.

The barrow becomes impossible to lift.

It is day until the very end of day.

Hunger. Fever. Thirst.

It is day until evening.

The small of the back is a knot of pain.

It is day until night.

Hands frozen, feet frozen.

It is day on the marsh where the sun makes the distant shapes of the trees sparkle in their shroud of hoar frost.

It is day for a whole eternity.

THE FAREWELL At noon they sent them out. In the corridor the blockhova snatched scarves off their heads, their coats. Tatters of scarves, tatters of coats.

It was a cold and dry winter day. One of those winter days when people say it would be nice to take a walk. People. Elsewhere.

The ground was covered with crusted snow.

Stripped of their coats, many were bare-armed. They folded their arms and rubbed their thin hands. Others protected their heads. No one had more than one-half inch of hair, no one had been there long. All were shivering violently. No defense against the cold.

The yard was too small to hold them, but they huddled together in the sunny part and pushed those who were dying into the shade. Seated in the snow they waited. And by their gaze one could see that they saw nothing, nothing of what surrounded them, nothing of the yard, nothing of the dying and the dead, nothing of themselves. They were there on the snow, seized with a shivering they could not control.

Suddenly, as if at a signal, they all began to scream. A scream that swelled, mounted, mounted, and spilled over the walls. Now they were only mouths that screamed, screamed at the sky. A flower bed of twisted mouths.

The screaming broke and in the silence one heard isolated sobs. They slumped down. Beaten down, resigned, perhaps. They were now only hollow eyes. A flower bed of hollow eyes.

Soon they could no longer bear accepting, resigning themselves. A wilder scream rose, rose and broke and silence fell again with sobs and the hollow eyes of despair.

Amid the motley rags and the throng of faces, those who were not weeping and not screaming no longer shivered.

And the screams began again.

Nothing heard these cries from the edge of terror. The world stopped far short of here. The world that says: "It would be nice to take a walk." Only our ears heard and we were already no longer alive. We were waiting for our turn.

The most recent silence lasts a long time. Are they all dead? No. They are still here. Defeated, and their conscious minds refuse still, refuse again, try to protest, defend themselves. The screams mount anew, mount and swell and spill over. And again they are only mouths screaming at the sky.

Silences and screams cut into the hours.

The sun withdraws. Shadow falls over the entire yard. There remains only a single illuminated row of faces that the last rays of the sun accentuate in their bony contours, twisted by cries.

Then one hears the rumbling of the trucks which screams immediately drown out. And when the gate opens, the yard becomes too big. All have risen and are huddling against the opposite wall, and in the cleared space, on the soiled snow, there are more corpses than one could have counted.

Two prisoners enter. At the sight of them the screaming grows louder than ever. It is the heaven commando.

Armed with clubs, they try to stampede the women toward the gate. The women do not move. Inert. Then they give in. Almost without being pushed, they come closer.

The first truck is backed right up to the gate.

A prisoner is standing on the truck, a giant in a jacket with an upturned fur collar, an astrakhan hat pulled down over his ears.

(Members of the heaven commando have privileges. They are well dressed, eat their fill. For three months. When this time runs out, others replace them and see them off. To heaven. To the oven. And so it goes every three months. They are the ones who keep the gas chambers and smokestacks running.)

On the back of his jacket we see a cross in red lead. The women have red crosses too; there are more and more striped dresses with them now.

The other two push the women toward him. He undoes his belt and grasps it securely at the ends, passes it under the arms of one woman after another and loads them. He throws them on the floor of the truck. When they come to, they get up. There are unalterable reflexes.

Up. Up. Another another. Up. Up. Another.

He works quickly, like one who knows his work, one who wants to do it better each time. The truck is full. Not enough. With a hard shove he packs and packs and then continues to load. The women are crushed against one another. They no longer cry out, no longer tremble.

When it is really impossible for him to pack in any more, he jumps down, lifts up the tailgate, attaches the chains. He casts a last glance at his work as though inspecting the job. He grabs a few more about the waist and throws them in on top of the others. The others get them on their heads, on their shoulders. They do not cry out, do not tremble. The loading completed, he gets in next to the driver. Let's go. The SS starts up.

Drexler is present at the send-off. Her hands on her hips, she supervises, like a foreman who supervises a job and is satisfied.

The women in the truck do not cry out. Jammed in, they attempt to work their arms or their bodies free. Incomprehensible that one should still want to free an arm, that one should want to brace oneself.

One has her chest thrust far over the side panel. Straight. Stiff. Her eyes gleam. She looks at Drexler with hatred, with scorn, a scorn that ought to kill. She did not scream with the others, her face is ravaged only by disease.

The truck starts up. Drexler follows it with her glance.

When the truck pulls away, she waves good-by and she laughs. She laughs. And she waves good-by for a long time.

This is the first time that we have seen her laugh.

Another truck backs up to the gate of block 25.

I no longer watch.

ROLL CALL When it drags on, there is something wrong. An error in the count or danger. What sort of danger? One never knows. Danger.

An SS approaches, whom we recognize instantly. The doctor. Right away the strongest ones inch forward, the bluest ones pinch their cheeks. He comes toward us, looks at us. Does he know what oppresses us as he looks at us?

He passes.

We begin to breathe again.

Farther on, he halts at the ranks of the Greek women. He asks: "Which are the women between twenty and thirty who have had a living child?"

It is necessary to replenish the guinea pigs in the experiment block.

The Greek women have just arrived.

We for our part have been here too long. A few weeks. Too thin or too weakened for them to cut open our bellies.

NIGHT The octopi were strangling us with their viscous muscles and we freed an arm only to be choked by a tentacle that wrapped itself around our necks, squeezed the vertebrae, squeezed them until they snapped. The vertebrae, the trachea, the esophagus, the larynx, the pharynx and all the passages of the throat, squeezed them till they broke. We had to free our throats and in order to save ourselves from strangulation, we had to sacrifice our arms, our legs, our waists to the clasping, intruding tentacles that multiplied endlessly, sprang up everywhere, so innumerable that we were tempted to give up the struggle and the exhausting vigilance. The tentacles unwound, unwound their threat. The threat hung poised a long moment and we were there hypnotized, incapable of beating a retreat in the face of this beast that was charging, coiling, clinging, crushing. We were about to succumb when we suddenly had the impression of waking up. They are not octopi, it is mud. We are swimming in mud, sticky mud with inexhaustible tentacles of waves. It is a sea of mud in which we must swim, swim vigorously, swim to exhaustion, till we run out of breath keeping our heads above the eddies of mud. We wince with disgust, mud gets into our eyes, our noses, into our mouths, chokes us and we flail with our arms to try to steady ourselves in this mud that engulfs us in octopus arms. And it would be bad enough to swim in the mud if we were not compelled to carry hand-barrows filled with clods of earth, so heavy that the load pulls us inescapably to the bottom, that is why the mud gets into our throats and into our ears, sticky, icy. Holding these barrows above our heads requires a superhuman effort and our comrade in front sinks, disappears, is swallowed up in the mud. It is necessary to pull her up, to get her to the surface of the mud, to let go of the barrow, impossible to get rid of it, it is chained to your fist so securely, so tightly that the two of us roll over locked in mortal combat, tied to one another by the barrow from which clods spill, getting mixed up with mud, that we splash in in a final attempt to free ourselves and the barrow is now filled with eyes and teeth, eyes that gleam, teeth that sneer and light up the mud the way phosphorescent madrepores light up deep waters, and all these eyes and all these teeth flash and yell, flash and bite, flash and bite everywhere and shriek: "Schneller, schneller, weiter, weiter," and when we punch these faces that are all teeth and eyes our fists meet only soft cataracts, rotten sponges. We want to save ourselves, swim out of this ooze. The mudbank is as crowded as a swimming pool on a summer afternoon, and everywhere we bump into running, oily masses that block all retreat and shoulders roll, turn, bump other shoulders. It is a jumble of bodies, a melee of arms and legs and when finally we think that we have reached solid ground it is really because we are pounding against the boards that we sleep on and everything vanishes into a shadow in which the leg that is moving belongs to Lulu, the arm belongs to Yvonne, the head on my chest that presses on me is Viva's head, and awakened by the sensation that I am at the edge of the void, at the edge of the tier, on the verge of falling out into the corridor, I plunge again into another nightmare, for this entire cave of shadow breathed, breathed and puffed, shaken in all its recesses by fitful sleep and thousands of nightmares. From the darkness emerges a shadow that glides, glides along the ground in the mud and runs toward the mouth of the cave and stirs others which glide and run and have difficulty finding their way in the dark, grope and hesitate, brush against one another, speak to one another in meaningless words: "Where are my shoes? Is that you? Dysentery, this is the third time I have gone tonight." Other shadows return, feel around for their places,

places for their heads touching other heads and from all the tiers nightmares rise, take shape in the shadows, from all the tiers rise the plaints and groans of bruised bodies that struggle with mud, with faces of shrieking hyenas: "Weiter, weiter," for hyenas shriek these words and our only recourse is to curl up and try to summon up a nightmare that is bearable, perhaps one in which we return home, in which we go back home and we say: "It's me, here I am, I'm back, you see," but all the members of the family that we had thought tormented with anxiety turn toward the wall, become silent, indifferent strangers. We say again: "It's me, I'm here, I know now that it is real, that I am not dreaming, I have dreamed so often that I was going back home and it was horrible to wake up, this time it is real, it is real because I am in the kitchen, because I am touching the sink. You see, Mama, it's me," and the coldness of the sink stone awakens me. It is a brick come loose from the wall that separates our cell from the next one where other larvae sleep and groan and dream under the blankets that cover them—those are shrouds that cover them for they are dead, today or tomorrow, it is all the same, they are dead to a return to the kitchen where their mothers await them. We feel ourselves teetering over a pit of shadow, a bottomless pit—it is the pit of night or of another nightmare, or our real death, and we struggle furiously, endlessly. We must go back, go back home to feel the sink stone with our hands and we fight against the vertigo that lures us to the bottom of the pit of night or of death, we make one last, desperate effort and we cling to the brick, the cold brick that we hold close to our heart, the brick that we have snatched from a pile of bricks stuck together with ice, chipping the ice with our nails, quick, quick, the clubs and the straps are flying—quick, quicker, our nails are bleeding—and this cold brick against our heart we carry to another pile, in a gloomy cortege in which each woman has a brick against her heart, for this is the way we carry bricks here, one brick after another, from morning till evening and it is not enough that we must carry bricks all day long at the construction site, we carry them again at night, for at night everything pursues us at once, the mud of the marsh in which we sink, the cold bricks that we must carry against our hearts, the kapos who shout and the dogs who can move on the mud as on solid ground and bite us at a signal from the flashing eyes in the darkness and we have the hot moist breath of the dog on our faces and fear beads our temples. And night is more exhausting than day, peopled with coughs and rattles, with those who are dying alone, pressed against the others who are at grips with mud, dogs, bricks and shouts, those whom we will find dead when we awake, whom we carry through the mud in front of our door, whom we will leave there rolled up in the blanket in which they yielded up their lives. And each dead woman is as light and as heavy as the shadows of the night, light in that she is wasted and heavy with an accumulation of sufferings that no one will ever share.

And when the whistle blows reveille, it is not that night is over

for night is over only when the stars pale and the sky takes on color,

it is not that night is over

for night is over only with the day,

when the whistle blows reveille there is the whole gap of eternity to cross over between night and day.

When the whistle blows reveille, it is one nightmare that is fixed, another nightmare that begins

there is only one moment of lucidity between the two, one in which we hear the beating of our hearts, listening to hear whether they have the strength to beat much longer, much longer that is to say days because our hearts cannot count in weeks or in months, we count in days and each day counts a thousand agonies and a thousand eternities.

The whistle blows in the camp, a voice cries: "Zell Appell" and we understand: "It is roll call," and another voice: "Aufstehen," and it is not the end of night

it is not the end of night for the women who are delirious in sick bay

it is not the end of night for the rats that attack their lips, still alive

it is not the end of night for the icy stars in the icy sky

it is not the end of night

it is the hour when shadows fade back into the walls, when other shadows go forth into the night

it is not the end of night

it is the end of a thousand nights and of a thousand nightmares.

UP TO FIFTY The man kneels down. Crosses his arms. Lowers his head. The kapo comes forward. He has his club. Comes up to the kneeling man and plants his feet firmly.

The SS comes over wih his dog.

The kapo raises his club, holding it in both hands, and delivers a blow across the small of the back. Eins.

Another. Zwei.

Another. Drei.

It is the man who counts. In the intervals between the strokes we hear him.

Vier.

Fünf. His voice grows faint.

Sechs.

Sieben.

Acht. We no longer hear him. But he is still counting. He must count up to fifty.

At each blow his body flinches a bit more. The kapo is tall and he uses all his height and strength in striking.

At each blow the dog yaps, wants to leap.

Its muzzle follows the trajectory of the club.

"Weiter," the anweiserin shouts at us because we are leaning motionless on our spades.

"Weiter." Our arms have dropped.

This man that they are beating with the noise of beating a rug.

He is still counting. The SS listens to see if he is still counting.

Fifty strokes of a club on a man's back are interminable.

We count. Let him count too! Let him keep on counting!

His head touches the ground. Each blow gives him a jolt that tears him apart. Each blow gives us a jolt.

The sound of fifty strokes of a club on a man's back is interminable.

If he were to stop counting, the strokes would stop and begin again at zero.

Fifty strokes of a club on a man's back are interminable and reverberate.

THE TULIP In the distance there is the outline of a house. In the squalls it makes one think of a boat, in winter. A boat at anchor in a northern port. A boat on the gray horizon.

We were walking with our heads lowered under squalls of sleet that lashed our faces, stung like hail. After each gust we feared the next one and bowed our heads still lower. The gust pelted, slapped, lacerated. A handful of coarse salt thrown full force into the face.

We continued on, pushing before us a cliff of wind and snow.

Where were we going?

This was a direction that we had never taken before. We had turned before the creek. The banked-up road skirted a lake, a big frozen lake.

Where were we heading? What could we do over here? The question that dawn asked us everyday at dawn. What work was waiting for us? Marsh, hand trucks, bricks, sand. We could not think of these words without our hearts sinking.

We marched. We interrogated the landscape. A steel-gray frozen lake. A landscape that does not reply.

The road swings away from the lake. The wall of wind and snow shifts to one side. It is here that the house comes into view. We march with less difficulty. We are going toward a house.

It is at the edge of the road. Red brick. The chimney is smoking. Who can be living in this isolated house? It draws nearer. We see white curtains. Muslin curtains. We say muslin with a sweet taste in our mouths. And in front of the curtains in the space between the window and the storm sash, there is a tulip.

Our eyes sparkle as though witnessing an apparition. "Did you see that? Did you see that? A tulip." All eyes are trained on the flower. A tulip here in this desert of ice and snow. Pink between two pale leaves. We look at it. We forget the pelting sleet. The column slows down. "Weiter," shouts the SS. Our heads are still turned toward the house that we have long since passed.

All day long we dream of that tulip. Sleet was falling, sticking to the backs of our soaked and frozen jackets. The day was long, as long as every day. At the bottom of the ditch that we were digging the tulip blossomed in its delicate corolla.

On the way back, long before coming to the house on the lake, our eyes were waiting for it. There it was, against the backdrop of the white curtains. A pink cup between the pale leaves. And during the roll call we said to comrades who were not with us: "We saw a tulip."

We never returned to that ditch. Others must have finished it. In the mornings at the crossing where the road to the lake branched off we had a moment of hope.

When we learned that it was the house of the SS who was in charge of the fishery, we hated our memory and the tenderness that they had not yet dried up within us.

MORNING From the edge of the darkness a voice shouted "Aufstehen." From the darkness a voice echoed "Stavache," and there was a dark stirring from which each withdrew her limbs. We had only to find our shoes and leap down. The strap whistled and lashed over those who did not emerge quickly enough from the blankets. The strap, in the hand of the stubhova standing in the passageway, flew up to the third tier, flew to the middle of the tiers, whipped faces, legs cramped by sleep. When everything was stirring and moving, when blankets everywhere were being shaken and folded, we heard the clink of metal against metal, steam veiled the flickering of the candle in the midst of the darkness. They were uncovering the canteens to serve tea. And the women who had just come in leaned against the wall, breathing hard, helping their hearts with their hands on their chests. They were returning from kitchens that were a long way off, a long way off when you carry an enormous canteen the handles of which cut into your palms. A long way off in the snow, in the ice or in the mud in which you go three steps forward, take two backward, go back, go forward, falling and getting up and falling again under a load too heavy for arms without strength. When they have caught their breath, they say: "It is cold this morning, colder than last night." They say "this morning." It is the middle of the night, a little after three o'clock.

The tea steams with a repulsive odor. The stubhovas dish it out stingily to our feverish thirsts. They keep the greater part of it for themselves to wash with. This is the best use to which it can be put, surely, and we too would like to wash up with good hot water. We have not washed since we arrived here, not even our hands with cold water. We drink our tea from our mess tins that smell of yesterday's soup.

There is no water for our mess tins either. Taking one's tea means getting it by force, in a melee of blows, jabs, punches, screams. Consumed by thirst and fever, we are spun around in the melee. We drink our tea standing, jostled by those who are afraid that they will not get theirs and by those who want to go out, because they must go out right away, as soon as they get up they must go out. The whistle blows the last call: "Alles raus."

The door is open to the stars. Each morning is colder than the last. Each morning we have the feeling that if we have borne it up to now, now it is too much, we cannot go on. At the threshold of the stars we hesitate, we would like to pull back. Then the clubs, the straps and the shouts fly fast. The first women near the door are driven out into the cold. From the depths of the block, under the rain of blows a crush develops that drives everyone out into the cold.

Outside is exposed ground, piles of stones, piles of dirt, so many obstacles to skirt, ditches to avoid, with ice, slush or snow and the excrement of the night. Outside, the cold penetrates, penetrates to the bone. We are transfixed by the cold. By icy stabs. Outside the night is clear and cold. The shadows cast by the moon are blue on the ice or on the snow.

It is roll call. All the blocks yield up their shadows. With movements stiff from cold and fatigue a crowd stumbles toward the Lagerstrasse. The crowd is organized into ranks of five in a confusion of shouts and blows. It takes a long time for all these shadows to line up, losing their footing on the ice, in the slush or in the snow, all these shadows who seek out one another and draw near each other to present the least surface to the icy wind.

Then silence reigns.

With her neck retracted into her shoulders, her chest pulled in, each woman puts her hands under the arms of the woman

71

in front of her. In the first row, they cannot do this, and they are rotated. Chest to back, we stand huddled together and although we thus set up a common circulation for all, a common circulatory system, we are all frozen. Annihilated by the cold. Our feet which remain distant, cut-off extremities, cease to exist. Our shoes were still damp from yesterday's snow or slush, from all the yesterdays. They never dry out.

We must stand motionless for hours in the cold and in the wind. We do not speak. The words freeze on our lips. The cold throws a whole nation of women who stand motionless into a stupor. In the night. In the cold. In the wind.

We stand motionless and the amazing thing is that we are still standing. Why? No one thinks "What is the use" or else does not say it. With our last bit of strength, we stand.

I stand in the midst of my comrades and I think that if I return one day and want to explain this inexplicable thing, I will say: "I used to say to myself: you must stand, you must stand for the entire roll call. You must stand again today. It is because you will have stood again today that you will return, if you do return one day." And this will be false. I did not say anything to myself. I did not think anything. The will to resist no doubt lay in a much deeper and more secret mechanism which has since broken; I shall never know. And if the dead had demanded of those who returned that they give an account, they would be incapable of doing so. I did not think anything. I did not look at anything. I did not feel anything. I was a skeleton of cold, with the cold blowing through all the gaps between the ribs of a skeleton.

I am standing in the midst of my comrades. I do not look at the stars. They stab with the cold. I do not look at the barbed-wire fences lit up white in the dark. They are claws of cold. I do not look at anything. I see my mother with the mask of resolute will that her face has become. My mother. Far away. I do not look at anything. I do not think anything.

Each whiff of air inhaled is so cold that it stings the whole respiratory system. The cold strips us. Skin ceases to be the tight protective envelope that it is to the body, even to the warmth of the belly. The lungs crack in the icy wind. Wash on a line. My heart is contracted, pinched, pinched till it hurts, and suddenly I feel something snap there in my heart. My heart breaks loose from my chest and from all that surrounds it and supports it. I feel a stone dropping within me, dropping with a thud. It is my heart. And a marvelous sense of well-being invades me. How comfortable it is to be rid of this fragile and demanding heart. One slips into a state of elation which must be that of happiness. Everything melts inside me, everything takes on the fluidity of happiness. I surrender and it is sweet to surrender to death, sweeter than surrendering to love and it is sweet to know that it is the end, the end of suffering and struggling, the end of asking the impossible of a heart that can bear no more. The giddiness lasts less than an instant, long enough to attain a bliss that we did not know existed.

And when I come to, it is to the jolting slaps that Viva is giving me across the cheeks, with all her might, setting her mouth and averting her eyes. Viva is strong. She does not faint at roll call. I do every morning. It is a moment of ineffable bliss. Viva must never know this.

She calls and calls my name which comes to me from far away from unfathomable emptiness—it is the voice of my mother that I hear. The voice grows hard: "Heads up. On your feet." And I feel that I cling to Viva as much as a child clings to its mother. I cling to the woman who has kept me from falling into the slush, into the snow from which one does not get up again. And I must struggle to make a choice between this consciousness that is suffering and this surrender that was bliss, and I choose because Viva says to me: "Heads up. On your feet." I do not dispute her order, but I do want to give in once, just once because that will be the only time. It is so easy to die here. One has only to let one's heart go.

I regain possession of myself, I regain possession of my body as of a garment that one puts on, cold from the dampness, of my pulse that is returning and beating, of my lips seared by the cold, the corners chapped and ragged. I regain possession of the anguish that makes its home in me and of the hope that I have been violating.

Viva lays her hard voice aside and asks: "Are you feeling better?" and her voice is so reassuring in its tenderness that I answer: "Yes, Viva. I am feeling better." It is my lips that respond, cracking a bit more around the cold and fever sores.

I am in the midst of my comrades. I take my place once more in the poor communal warmth that our contact creates and since I must come to, I return to the roll call and I think: this is the morning roll call—what a poetic title that would be—this is the morning roll call. I no longer know whether it is morning or evening.

This is the morning roll call. The sky gradually takes on color in the east. A sheaf of flames fans out, icy flames and the shadow that blots out our shadows dissolves bit by bit and faces form out of these shadows. All of these faces are purplish and ghastly pale, more pronouncedly purplish and pale as the sky lightens. And we distinguish now between those whom death has taken last night and those that it will take tonight. For death is painted on their faces, marked there inexorably and there is no need for our eyes to meet to realize at a glance that Suzanne Rose is going to die, that Mounette is going to die. Death is marked on the skin stuck

74

to their cheeks, on the skin stuck to their eye sockets, on the skin stuck to their jawbones. And we know that it would be of no use now to evoke their home or their sons or their mothers. It is too late. We can do nothing more for them.

The shadow dissolves a bit more. The barking of the dogs draws closer. It is the SS approaching. The blockhovas shout "silence" in their impossible languages. The cold nips our hands as they move out from under our arms. Fifteen thousand women stand at attention.

The SS pass by—tall in their black cloaks, boots, high black hoods. They pass by and count. And it takes a long time.

When they have passed by, each woman puts her hands back in the hollows of another woman's armpits. The coughs held back until now burst forth and the blockhovas shout "Silence" to the coughs in their impossible language. We still must wait, wait for day.

Shadows dissolve. The sky turns to flame. Now we see fantastic corteges pass. Little Rolande asks: "Let me through to the front row, I want to see." Later she will say: "I was sure I recognized her, she had deformed feet, I was sure I recognized her by her feet." Her mother had gone to the sick bay a few days earlier. Each morning she watched in order to determine what day her mother had died.

Fantastic corteges pass by. These are the nightly dead that they take out of the sick bay to carry to the morgue. They are naked on stretchers roughly made of branches, stretchers that are too short. Their legs—the shinbones—hang down with their feet at the end, thin and bare. The head dangles over the other edge, bony and shaven. A ragged blanket is thrown across the middle. Four prisoners carry the stretchers, one at each handle, and it is true that one goes out feet first, this is always the way they carry them. They walk with difficulty in the snow or in the slush. They are going to fling the body on the pile near 25, bring back the empty, scarcely less heavy stretcher and pass by again with another body. Day in, day out this is their full-time job.

I watch them pass by and I stiffen. Just now I was surrendering to death. Each day at dawn, the temptation. When the stretcher goes by I stiffen. I want to die but not to be carried out on that little stretcher. Not to be carried out on that little stretcher with my feet dangling and my head dangling, naked under the ragged blanket. I do not want to be carried out on that little stretcher.

Death reassures me: I would not feel it. "You are not afraid of the crematorium, so why be afraid?" How kindred to us is death. Those who painted it with a hideous face had never seen it. Repulsion wins out. I do not want to be carried out on that little stretcher.

Then I know that all those who pass pass for me, that all those who die die for me. I watch them go by and say no. Allow yourself to slip into death, here in the snow. Let yourself slip away. No, because there is the little stretcher. I do not want to be carried out on the little stretcher.

The shadows dissolve completely. It is colder. I hear my heart and I talk to it as Arnolphe talked to his. I talk to it.

When will the day come when this authority over a heart, lungs, muscles will cease? The day when this forced solidarity of brain, of nerves, of bones and of every organ in the belly will be over? When will the day come when we will no longer be conscious of ourselves, my heart and I?

The redness in the sky fades and the whole sky blanches and far off in the pale sky crows appear that swoop down black over the camp in dense flocks. We wait for the end of roll call.

We wait for the end of roll call in order to go to work.

76

WEITER The SS at the four corners stake out limits that we must not cross. This was a big construction site. Everything was here that haunted us during the night: rocks to break, a road to pave, sand to excavate, hand-barrows for carrying gravel and sand, ditches to dig, bricks to carry from one pile to another. Assigned to various gangs with the Polish women, we exchanged sad smiles when we passed one another.

After the sun began to shine, it was less cold. At the midday break we sat down to eat on some building materials. Once the soup had been gulped down—it only took a couple of minutes, the longest part was the distribution, the waiting in line in front of the canteen—we had a bit of time left before returning to the gravel, to the sand, to the road, to the ditch, and to the bricks. We picked lice off the open collars of our dresses. This was where they swarmed in greatest number. Considering their numbers, killing a few hardly changed anything. It was our recreation. Sad. The midday rest period when we could sit down because the weather was fair.

Clustered in little groups of friends, we talked. Each woman told the name of her home province, where she lived, invited the others to pay her a visit. You will come, won't you? You will come. We promised. We made so many trips.

"Weiter." The shout breaks the lull of our daydreams.

"Weiter." To whom is he talking?

"Weiter."

A woman heads toward the stream. Her mess tin is in her hand, no doubt she wants to wash it. She stops, uncertain.

"Weiter." Is it addressed to her?

"Weiter." In the voice of the SS there is a note of mockery.

The woman hesitates. Ought she really go farther? Is it not permitted to go near the stream in this spot?

"Weiter." The SS orders more imperiously.

The woman backs off, stops again. Standing against the background of the marsh, every bit of her asks: "Is it permitted here?"

"Weiter," screams the SS.

Then the woman walks. She goes upstream.

"Weiter."

A shot. The woman crumples.

The SS slings his gun back onto his shoulder, whistles to his dog, goes toward the woman. Leaning over her, he turns her over the way one turns game over.

The other SS laugh from their posts.

She had overstepped the limit by less than twenty paces.

We count ourselves. Are we all here?

When the SS raised his gun and took aim, the woman was walking in the sunlight.

She was killed instantly.

She was a Polish woman.

Some have not seen anything and ask questions. Others wonder if they did see and say nothing.

THIRST

Thirst is an explorer's tale, you know, in the books we read as children. It is in the desert. People who see mirages and walk toward the unattainable oasis. They are without water for three days. The pathetic chapter in the book. At the end of the chapter, the supply caravan arrives, it had gone astray on the trails obliterated by the sandstorm. The explorers break open the water bags, they drink. They drink and are no longer thirsty. It is thirst from the sun, from the warm wind. The desert. A palm tree in filigree against the red sands.

But the thirst of the marsh is more burning than that of the desert. The thirst of the marsh lasts for weeks. The water bags never come. Reason wavers. Reason is laid low by thirst. Reason holds out against everything, but it gives in to thirst. In the marsh, no mirage, no hope of an oasis. Mud, mud. Mud and no water.

There is morning thirst and evening thirst.

There is day thirst and night thirst.

In the morning on awakening, lips speak and no sound comes from them. Anguish grips one's whole being, an anguish as stabbing as that of dreams. Is it the same as being dead? The lips try to speak, the mouth is paralyzed. The mouth forms no words when it is dry, when it has no more saliva. And the gaze wanders listlessly, it is the gaze of madness. The others say: "She is mad, she went mad during the night," and they resort to words that are supposed to reawaken reason. One would have to explain to them. The lips refuse. The muscles of the mouth want to attempt the articulatory movements but do not articulate. And it is despair born of my inability to tell them of the anguish that has choked me, the feeling of being dead and knowing it.

As soon as I hear them rattling, I run to the tea canteens.

They are not the water bags of the caravan. Quarts and quarts of herb tea, but divided into tiny portions, one each, and everyone else is still drinking when I am finished. My mouth is not even moistened and still the words refuse to come. My cheeks stick to my teeth, my tongue is hard, stiff, my jaws are blocked and still this feeling of being dead, of being dead and knowing it. And terror grows in my eyes. I feel terror growing in my eyes to the point of madness. Everything is sinking, everything is slipping away. Reason no longer exercises control. Thirst. Am I breathing? I am thirsty. Must I go out for roll call? I get lost in the crowd, I do not know where I am going. I am thirsty. Is it colder, or less cold? I do not feel it. I am thirsty, thirsty enough to scream. And the finger that I rub over my gums proves the dryness of my mouth. My will power crumbles. There remains one obsession: to drink.

And if the blockhova sends me to her quarters for her book, when I come upon the basin of soapy tea in which she has washed herself, my first thought is to brush off the dirty suds, to kneel down next to the basin and drink from it as a dog laps up water with its supple tongue. I recoil. From the soapy tea in which they have washed their feet. On the verge of insanity, I see how close thirst has come to making me lose my senses.

I go back to the roll call. And to my obsession. To drink. If only we would take the road to the right. There is a stream with a little bridge. To drink. My eyes see nothing, nothing but the stream, that far-off stream with the entire roll call lying between me and it, and the roll call is farther to cross than the Sahara. The column forms to march off. To drink. I get on the outside of the ranks, on the side from which the bank is easiest to reach.

The stream. Long before getting there, I am ready to

bound like an animal. Long before the stream is visible, I have my mess tin in my hand. And when the stream is there, it is necessary to leave the ranks, run forward, climb down the slippery bank. It is sometimes frozen, break the ice quickly, fortunately the cold is less intense, it is not thick, break the ice quickly with the edge of the mess tin, get water, and climb up the slippery bank, run to get back in place, eager eyes on the water which I spill if I run too fast. The SS runs over to me. He shouts. His dog runs in front of him, almost catches me. My comrades grab me and the ranks swallow me up. Greedy eyes on the water that splashes as I walk, I do not see the anxiety on their faces, the anxiety that I have caused them. My absence had seemed interminable to them. To drink. I was not afraid. To drink. As they do every morning, they say that it is madness to go down to the stream with the SS and his dog after me. He had had a Polish woman mauled to death the other day. And besides it is swamp water, it is water that carries typhoid. No, it is not swamp water. I drink. Nothing is more awkward than drinking out of a shallow mess tin while walking. The water splashes from one side to the other, dribbles down my lips. I drink. No, it is not swamp water, it is a stream. I do not answer because I cannot speak yet. It is not swamp water, but it has the taste of rotted leaves, and I have this taste in my mouth today whenever I think of this water, even when I am not thinking of it. I drink. I drink and I feel better. Saliva returns to my mouth. Words return to my lips, but I do not speak. Sight returns to my eyes. Life returns. I rediscover my breathing, my heart. I know that I am alive. I slowly suck my saliva. Lucidity returns, and sight—and I see little Aurore. She is ill, worn out by fever, her lips discolored, her eyes haggard. She is thirsty. She does not have the strength to climb down to the stream. And no one wants to go for her. She should not drink that dirty water, she is ill. I see her and I think: She could easily drink that water since she is going to die anyway. Every morning she comes next to me. She hopes that I will leave her a few drops of water in the bottom of the mess tin. Why would I give her some of my water? She is going to die anyway. She waits. Her eyes beg and I do not look at her. I feel her thirsty eyes on me, the pain in her eyes when I put the mess tin back in my belt. Life returns to me and I feel ashamed. And every morning I remain insensitive to her begging glance and her lips discolored by thirst, and every morning I feel ashamed after drinking.

My mouth is moistened. I could talk now. I do not talk. I would like this saliva to last a long while in my mouth. And the obsession: When shall I drink again? Will there be water where we will be working? There is never any water. It is the marsh. The marsh of mud.

My comrades thought me mad. Lulu used to tell me: "Watch out. You know very well that you always have to be on your guard here. You'll get yourself killed." I did not hear her. They never left my side and among themselves they would say: "We must look out for C., she is mad. She does not see the kapos or the SS or the dogs. She just stands there with an empty look on her face instead of working. She does not understand when they shout, she wanders off anywhere. They will kill her." They were afraid for me, they were afraid to look at me with the wild eyes that I had. They thought me mad and no doubt I was. I do not remember anything of those weeks. And during those weeks which were the hardest, so many of us died that I liked and I did not recall that I had learned of their deaths.

On the days when we take the other direction, away from the stream, I do not know how I am able to bear the disappointment.

There is morning thirst and afternoon thirst.

Since morning, I have thought only of drinking. When the midday soup is served, it is salty, so salty it strips raw the mouth burning with canker sores. "Eat. You must eat." So many had died already who had refused food. "Try. It is rather watery today." "No, it is salty." I push away the spoonful that I have tried to swallow. Nothing can go down when there is no saliva in the mouth.

Sometimes we go to the hand trucks. A demolition site with scraggy bushes between the ruined houses. They are covered with frost. With each barrow of rocks I carry to the truck, I brush past a bush from which I pluck a small twig. I lick the frost and this makes no water in my mouth. As soon as the SS moves away, I race toward the clean snow, there is a bit left like a sheet stretched out to dry. I take a handful of snow, and the snow makes no water in my mouth.

If I pass by the open cistern on the ground, giddiness seizes me, my head spins. I do not throw myself in because I am with Carmen or Viva. And each time we pass by they try to make a wide detour. But I drag them on, they follow me so as not to let me escape and at the edge they pull me back roughly.

During the break, the Polish women gather around the cistern and scoop up water in a mess tin lowered on a wire. The wire is too short. The woman leaning over it almost all the way inside the cistern, her comrades hold her by the legs. She raises a bit of cloudy water in the bottom of the mess tin and she drinks. Another takes a turn at drawing water. I approach them and I make them understand that I would like some. The mess tin goes down at the end of the wire, the Polish woman leans over as though she were going to fall, brings up another bit of water which she hands to me saying: "Kleba?" I have no bread. I give away all my bread in the evening to get tea. I answer that I have no bread, with a plea on my lips. She tips over the tin and the water spills. I would have fallen had Carmen or Viva not run up to me.

When we are in the marsh, the whole day I think of the way back, of the stream. But the SS remembers this morning. At the bend from which we can see the little bridge, he goes forward. He goes down to the stream and makes his dog wade in it. When we get there the water is muddy and foul. I would get some anyway, but it is impossible. All the anweiserins are on the edge. This is the cruelest thing an SS can do. I would rather be beaten.

There is afternoon thirst and there is evening thirst.

In the evening, during the whole roll call, I think of the tea that they are going to hand out. I am one of the first to be served. Thirst makes me bold. I push to get ahead of the others. I drink and when I have drunk I am still more thirsty. This herb tea does not quench thirst.

I now have my bread in my hand, my piece of bread and the few grams of margarine that constitute our evening ration. I hold them in my hand and I offer them from cell to cell to anyone who would swap their portion of tea for them. I dread that no one will do this. There is always someone who takes it. Every evening I exchange my bread for a few gulps. I drink it straight down and I am still more thirsty. When I return to our tier, Viva says to me: "I saved my tea for you—it's neither real tea nor herb tea—it will be for just before you go to sleep." She cannot make me wait that long. I drink and I am still thirsty. And I think of the water of the stream that the dog spoiled earlier, that I might have had a full tin of, and now I am thirsty, thirstier still.

There is evening thirst and there is night thirst, the worst of all. Because at night I drink, I drink and the water instantly becomes dry and hard in my mouth. And the more I drink, the more my mouth fills with rotten leaves that harden.

Or else it is an orange section. It gives between my teeth and it is really an orange section—unheard of that one should find oranges here—it is really an orange section. I have the taste of orange in my mouth, the juice seeps under my tongue, touches my palate, my gums, trickles down my throat. It is a slightly sour orange and wonderfully cool. This taste of orange and the sensation of cold wake me up. The awakening is dreadful. But the second when the orange peel gives between my teeth is so delightful that I would like to summon up that dream. I chase after it, I force it. But again it is the taste of rotted leaves like drying mortar. My mouth is dry. Not bitter. When there is a bitter taste in the mouth, it means one has not lost the sense of taste, it means that one still has saliva in one's mouth.

THE HOUSE

It was raining. A screen of rain shut off the plain. We had been walking a long time. The road was a mess of puddles. When we were tempted to go around them the anweiserins screamed: "Formation. Keep the formation," and they shove into the mud those women who hesitated because of their shoes. No description can give an idea of the shoes that we had.

We had come to a big plowed field. We had to pull out the quackgrass roots turned up by the plow. Stooping over, we pulled out the whitish strands and put them in our aprons. This felt cold and damp against the belly. Heavy too. At the end of the field we emptied our aprons and started another furrow. It was raining. Bending over the furrows, furrow after furrow. The rain soaked our clothing through. We were naked. An icy streamlet formed between the shoulder blades and ran down to the small of the back. We no longer paid any attention to it. But the hand that pulled out the quackgrass was dead. And the mud stuck more and more to our shoes which were getting heavy, heavier and heavier to pick off the ground. It had been raining since morning.

The anweiserins had taken shelter under a lean-to made of branches. They shouted from a distance. When we were at the far end of the field we no longer heard them. We dawdled there a bit. We could have pretended to work. In any case we had to stoop down over the furrows, they could see us. Besides it was too painful to straighten up.

We moved two by two. We talked as we walked. We were talking about the past and the past became unreal. We talked still more about the future and the future became a certainty. We made many plans. We made them endlessly.

At noon the rain was falling twice as hard. We could no

longer see the field which had been transformed into a sea of mud.

Farther off there was an abandoned house. This house was not for us. The SS was already whistling for us to re-form the ranks, after the break. We were resigned to returning to the quackgrass roots, to the muddy clods. But the column left the field behind. Geneviève said: "I wish they would let us take shelter in the house." She had formulated the wish that all of us had. Expressing it showed how unrealistic it was. All the same, we are heading toward the house. We are quite close. The column stops. An SS shouts that we are going to go in but that if we make any noise we will leave immediately. Should we believe this?

We go into the house as though into a church. It is a peasant cottage which they have begun to tear down. They tear down all the peasant cottages, rip out the hedges and the fences, level the gardens into one vast holding. That is how they get rid of small farming here. The farmers were liquidated first. The house is marked with a "J" in black print. Jews lived here.

We go into a smell of damp plaster. The floor boards and the wallpaper have been stripped. Practically all the doors and windows too. We sit down on the rubble. We feel the cold from our dresses and our jackets even more. The first arrivals get places along the walls, they lean back. Others squeeze in wherever they can.

We look at the house as though we had forgotten and were rediscovering words. "It is a rather nice room."—"Yes, it has good light."—"The table must have been there."—"Or the bed."—"No, this is the dining room. See the wallpaper." There is a scrap of wallpaper still hanging. "I would put a couch here next to the fireplace."—"Some cottage curtains would look nice. You know those prints."

We provide the house with all its furniture, polished, comfortable, familiar. It is complete except for a few details. "There should be a radio next to the couch."—"They use storm windows here. You can grow cactuses."—"Do you like cactuses? I prefer hyacinths. You put the bulbs in water and you have flowers before spring."—"I don't like the smell of hyacinths."

The anweiserins have settled down in the other room. The SS are drowsing beside them. We are huddled against one another. Our body heat makes our clothing steam in clouds that rise toward the holes in the windows. The house becomes warm, lived in. We are comfortable. We stare at the rain wishing that it would last till evening.

EVENING At the sound of the whistle we have to lay down our implements, clean them, and stack them in a neat pile.—Form ranks.—Keep quiet.—Don't move.—Anweiserins and kapos make the count. Are they in error? Recount.—Scream.—Two short. Remember. They are the two from this afternoon. The two who collapsed by their spades. The furies immediately swooped down and beat them and beat them. One does not get used to seeing people beaten. The blows were to no avail. The spades slipped from their hands drained of blood, life left their eyes and their eyes did not implore. Their eyes were mute. The furies went after the two women tooth and nail although they no longer stirred. If they no longer react to the blows, it is because there is nothing left for them to do. Take them away. We had carefully carried them along the slope to a place where the grass was dry and we had returned to our spades.

They are missing now. Not everyone knows, they ask questions. The names pass from mouth to mouth in a whispering not tinged with any emotion. We are too tired. Berthe and Anne-Marie are dead. Berthe, which one was she? Berthe from Bordeaux. They had been counted this morning when we left, they must be counted when we return. We must carry them. No one moves. Involuntarily, each woman lowers her head, would like to melt into the mass, not be noticed, give no sign. So worn out that they calculate with alarm the little they can still get from their legs. The majority can walk only by leaning on the arm of someone else. The anweiserins move back through the ranks, examine faces and feet. They will pick out the strongest. Women leaning on others who are not so weak dread the possibility that these last will be selected. How shall they get back if the arms that support them are taken away?

The anweiserins look for the best shod, the tall ones. "Du. Du. Du," as they call three. Then others volunteer. We disengage ourselves and go toward the dead women. How are we to pick them up? The anweiserins indicate that each woman is to pick up a limb. And quick.

We bend over our companions. They are not yet rigid. When we grasp their ankles and wrists, their bodies sag, sag to the ground and it is impossible to hold them up. It would be better to carry them by the shoulders and the knees but we cannot get a firm grip. Finally we succeed. We take our places at the end of the column. They are still counting. The number comes out right this time. The column starts moving.

There are several kilometers to go. Five at least.

The column has started.

At first it is Berthe and Anne-Marie that we are carrying. Soon they are nothing more than very heavy bundles that slip out of our grasps at every movement. From the very start we fall behind. We ask women to pass the word along to the front rank to slow down. The column moves on as fast as ever. The kapo is up front. She has good shoes. She is in a hurry.

The SS follow us. They shuffle their boots because we move so slowly. The anweiserin laughs with them. She shows them dance steps, making foul jokes the while. They are enjoying themselves.

It is a pale and almost mild evening. Back home the trees must be in bud. An SS pulls out a harmonica from his pocket. He plays and our distress turns to discomfort.

We call for women to relieve us. No one hears. No one comes. No one feels strong enough to relieve us. We are more and more tired, bent, drawn.

Carmen spies some pieces of broken boards in the ditch.

We set down our comrades on the road in order to gather the boards. The SS wait. The second one takes out his knife and shaves the bark from the branch that he uses as a club. The anweiserin accompanies the harmonica. She sings "I will wait." Their favorite song.

We place each body across two boards. We grasp the ends of the boards and start off again. Carmen says: "You remember, Lulu, when mother would say to us: 'Don't touch that filthy wood. You'll get a splinter and a bad infection in your finger.'" Our mothers.

At first this seems more satisfactory, then the bodies slip, fold in the middle, fall. At each step we must shift this inert body and these boards. The SS take turns playing the harmonica, laughing and singing. They laugh loudly, the girl laughs louder still.

The column pulls farther ahead. We make an effort that we did not dream we were capable of. A truck comes. The column stops by the side of the road in order to let it pass. We take advantage of this to gain a little ground. The truck is the one that picks up the canteens in which they bring soup to the construction sites at noon. There are construction sites all around. In the distance all around there are heaps of shovels and spades. The driver stops the truck, talks to the SS. I am near the one with the harmonica. He is a kid. He looks about seventeen. The same age as my younger brother. I speak to him: "Couldn't we put our comrades on the truck going back to the camp?" His snicker insults us and he bursts out laughing. He laughs, laughs and finds this very funny. He is rocked with laughter and the other one imitates him and the girl does too, forcing her laugh as she slaps me. I am ashamed. How can one ask them for anything. The truck pulls away.

Enough of that now. They decide that it has gone on long

enough, enough of this nonchalance with romping dogs, slack leashes. They put away the harmonica, pull in the dogs and shout: "Schneller jetzt." We tense up. With the dogs at our heels we must now catch up with the column.

We must. We must.

We must . . . Why must we since it makes no difference to us if we die right now, killed by the dogs or by the clubs, here on the road in the pale evening. No. We must. Maybe because of their laughter just now, we must.

We manage to regain the column, almost reach it. We beg for someone to take our place. Two come. They replace the two weakest ones who are drooping from exhaustion. We change hands without breaking march. We have the dogs' muzzles at the backs of our legs. One sign, one shake of the leash, and they will bite. We walk with the bodies which slip, which we catch, which slip again. Their feet scrape the road, their heads dangle almost to the ground. We can no longer bear to see these faces, with their eyes rolled back. Berthe. Anne-Marie. With the hand that is not carrying we lift up the heads for a moment. We must stop. We must abandon these heads whose eyelids we did not have the courage to close.

We do not look because tears stream down our faces, stream down without our crying. The tears stream down from a weariness and helplessness. And we suffer in this dead flesh as if it were alive. The boards under their thighs scrape them, cut them. Berthe. Anne-Marie.

To keep their arms from dangling, we try to fold them on their chests. We would have to hold them there. Their arms hang down and strike our legs as we walk.

The SS behind us march smartly. The outing is over, they say. They hold the leashes taut. The dogs crowd closer. We do not turn. We try not to feel their muzzles, their hot and rapid breath, not to hear their four-footed gait, their canine gait with the irritating scratching of claws on the pebbles of the road. Not to hear the thud of the stick against us. There is no bark on it now, it is white and damp.

We walk, tensely. Our hearts thump, thump as if they were to burst and we think: my heart will not stand it, I will have heart failure. It has not failed yet, it is still holding up. For how many yards? Our anxiety breaks up the miles into paces, yards, light poles, bends in the road. We are forever mistaken about a pole or a bend in the road. This is the plain, the plain covered with marshes as far as the eye can see where there are no landmarks, occasionally a clump of vegetation reddened by the frost that constantly lends itself to confusion with another. And despair crushes us.

But we must. We must.

We are drawing near. The nearness of the camp can be sensed by its odor. The smell of carrion, the smell of diarrhea that is overlaid by the thicker, more suffocating smell of the crematorium. When we are there, we do not smell it. When we return in the evening, we wonder how we can breathe this stench.

From this spot, the spot where the smell is recognizable, there are about three kilometers left.

After the little bridge, the pace quickens. Two more.

How we made them, I do not know. At the entrance our column has stopped to let others go first. We set down our burdens. When we had to pick them up again, we thought that we could not.

At the gate, we stood tall. We set our jaws, we looked up. It was a promise that we had made to one another, Viva and I. Our heads up high in front of Drexler, in front of Taube. We had even said: "Heads up high or feet first." O Viva!

The SS who was counting as we passed questions with her

stick. "Zwei Französinnen," the anweiserin answers disgustedly.

We carry our comrades to roll call. That makes two rows that spoil the alignment: the four bearers and the dead women lying in front of them.

The Jewish work gangs come back in their turn. They have two tonight. Like us. They have some every night. They have put them on doors removed from the houses they are knocking down and they have lifted the doors up on their shoulders. They are disfigured by the effort. We are sorry for them. We are so sorry that we sob. The dead are laid out quite flat, their faces toward the sky. We think: if only we had had some doors.

Roll call was as long as usual. To us it seemed shorter. Our hearts filled our chests and beat loud, loud and that kept us company like a watch when one is alone. And we listened to these hearts that were drowning everything else out, which little by little returned to their niches, settled in again and slackened their beat, slackened their beat and grew softer. And when we could once again hear them at just their usual tempo we were as disturbed as if we were at the edge of solitude.

At that moment our hands wiped away our tears.

Roll call lasted until the searchlights lit up the barbed wire, until night.

During the whole course of roll call, we did not look at them.

A corpse. The left eye gnawed by a rat. The other eye open with its fringe of lashes.

Try to look. Try to see.

A man who can no longer follow. The dog seizes him by the rump. The man does not stop. He walks with the dog walking behind him, on two legs, its muzzle at the man's rump.

The man walks. He has not uttered a cry. Blood stains the stripes on his trousers. From within, a stain that spreads as if on blotting paper.

The man walks with the dog's teeth in his flesh.

Try to look. Try to see.

A woman whom two people drag by the arms. A Jewess. She does not want to go to 25. The two drag her. She resists. Her knees scrape the ground. Her garment pulled by the sleeves rides up on her neck. Her trousers—a pair of men's trousers—have come undone, drag behind her inside out, held on by her ankles. A flayed frog, her loins naked, her buttocks with hollows of emaciation soiled with blood and pus. She shrieks. Her knees are rubbed raw against the gravel.

Try to look. Try to see.

AUSCHWITZ   This city which we were passing
through
was a strange city.
The women wore hats
hats set on curled hair.
They had shoes and stockings too
as in the city.
None of the inhabitants of this city
had a face
and so as not to show this
all turned away from us when we passed
even a child who held in his hand
a milk can as tall as his legs
violet enameled
and who ran away when he saw us.
We looked at these faceless beings
And it was we who were astonished.
We were disappointed too
we were hoping to see fruits and vegetables in the shops.
There were no shops either
only show windows
in which I would have been willing to recognize myself
in the ranks that were slipping over the panes.
I raised an arm
but all wished to recognize themselves
all raised their arms
and no one knew which one she was.
There was the time on the face of the station clock
we were glad to look at it
the time was true
and we were relieved to arrive at the beet silos
where we were going to work
on the far side of the town
that we had passed through like a morning sickness.

THE DUMMY

On the far side of the road, there is a field where the SS go to train their dogs. We see them go there with their dogs which they have fastened, two on a leash. The SS who goes first carries a dummy. It is a big doll dressed like us. A faded, dirty striped suit with sleeves that are too long. The SS holds it by one arm. He lets the feet drag and scrape the gravel. They have even put canvas boots on its feet.

Do not look. Do not look at this dummy trailing along the ground. Do not look at yourself.

SUNDAY On Sunday roll call was not so early. Not so long till daybreak. On Sunday the columns did not go out. We worked inside the camp. Sunday was the worst day of all.

One Sunday the weather was very fair. The sun rose in the sky without redness, without sheets of fire. The day started out blue right away, like a spring day. The sun, too, was like a spring sun. Do not think about home, about the garden, about the first outing of the season. Do not think. Do not think.

Here the difference between fair weather and bad weather was that there was dust instead of snow or slush, that the stench became fouler, the countryside more desolate in sunlight than in snow, more hopeless.

The end of roll call sounds. We must keep ranks which start slowly toward block 25. Every Sunday was different. To block 25. Why? We are afraid. Someone says: "Block 25 isn't big enough for everyone. We must be going directly to the gas chambers," and we pull ourselves together.

What are they going to do? We wait. We wait a long time. Until some men come, some men with shovels. They head toward the ditch. During the week, the ditch that separates the barbed wire from the inside of the camp had been deepened. Are there too many suicides? Those are the shots that we hear in the night. When a woman goes near the barbed wire, the guard on the watchtower fires before she can touch it. Why the ditch then?

Why all this?

The men are in their places, along the ditch, shovels in hand.

The columns stretch out in single file. Thousands of women in one file. An endless file. We follow. What are the

100

ones in front of us doing? We see them pass in front of the men, hold out their aprons. Into them the men dump two shovelfuls of dirt scooped from the ditch they have dug. What are we doing with this dirt? We follow. They begin to run. We run. Now blows from clubs and straps fall thick and fast. We try to protect our faces, our eyes. The blows fall on the backs of our necks, on our backs. Schnell. Schnell. Run.

On each side of the file, kapos and anweiserins scream. Schneller. Schneller. Scream and strike.

We have our aprons filled, and we run.

We run. We must keep in line, no straggling.

We run.

The gate.

This is where the furies are mainly concentrated. SS in skirts and in britches have joined the others. Run.

Past the gate, go to the left, step onto a plank precariously balanced between the sides of a ditch. Cross over the plank at a run. Blows before and after.

Run. Empty out the aprons in the spot indicated by the shouting.

Others with rakes level off the transported earth.

Run. Skirt the barbed wire. Do not brush against it, the current is on.

Once again pass through the gate to return. The passage is narrow. We must run even faster. Too bad for the women who fall there, they are trampled.

Run. Schneller. Run.

Return to the men who fill our aprons again with dirt.

They must do this quickly, they are being beaten. Heaping shovelfuls, they are being beaten, we are being beaten.

Our aprons filled, blows from clubs. Schneller.

Run toward the gate, run the gauntlet of straps and whips,

run over the plank that shifts and sags. Watch out for the cane of the chief SS who stands at the end of the plank. Empty one's apron under a rake, run, pass through the gate, through the more and more constricted passage—the club-wielders crowd around the outlet—run toward the men to pick up two more shovelfuls of dirt, run to the gate, in an endless loop.

They want to make a garden at the entrance to the camp.

Two shovelfuls of dirt is not very heavy. It gets heavier as you go on. It gets heavier and makes our arms stiff. We take a chance and hold the edges of our aprons carelessly so that a bit of dirt spills out. If a fury sees this, she will kill us. We do it just the same, it is too heavy.

Among the men there is a Frenchman. We scheme and time our rounds so that it is he who gives us dirt. We try to exchange a few words. He talks without moving his lips, without raising his eyes, the way one learns to speak in prison. Three rounds are required for one sentence.

The loop is not moving fast enough now. The furies scream louder, hit harder. Bottlenecks occur when women collapse and their comrades help them get up while others behind them, driven on by blows, want to keep on running. Also because the Jewish women think that they are taking more of a beating than we are and come to slip in between our striped dresses. They make trouble for us. They make trouble for us because of their clothes. They have no aprons. They were ordered to put their coats on backwards, buttoned down the back so that they could take the earth in the skirts of their coats which they gather up in a fold. They are a cross between scarecrows and penguins in their reversed sleeves that encumber their arms. And the women who have men's coats with vents. . . . A terrifying comedy.

We are sorry for them but we do not want to get sepa-

102

rated. We protect each other. Everyone wants to stay close to a friend, one woman to stay in front of a weaker one to take the blows for her, another to stay behind a woman who can no longer run to steady her if she falls.

The Frenchman has arrived recently. He is from Charonne. The Resistance is spreading in France. We would brave anything to talk with him.

Run to the gate—schnell—pass through—weiter—teeter on the plank over the ditch—schneller—empty our aprons—run—look out for the barbed wire—again the gate there is always some woman we step on that is where the officer with the cane is standing now—run up to the men—stretch out our aprons—blows—run toward the gate. A delirious race.

We think of slipping off and hiding in one of the blocks. Impossible, every way out is guarded by clubs. The women who try to force their way through the cordon are mauled.

It is forbidden to go to the latrines. It is forbidden to stop for an instant.

In the beginning, slowing down is more painful than keeping up the pace. At the least slow-up the blows increased in fury. Later, we would prefer to be beaten and not to run, our legs no longer obey. But the minute we slow down, the blows fall so hard that we start running again.

Some women fall. The furies take them out of the line and drag them to the gate of 25. Taube is there. The confusion mounts. There are more and more Jews among us. With each round our group splits up further. We manage to stay together by twos. These pairs do not split up, they stick together and they pull one another out when they get caught going through the entrance in the panic of those who are being trampled and of those who are afraid of stumbling over the others. A delirious race.

Some women fall. The round continues. Run. Keep running. Do not slow down. Do not stop. We do not look at the women who fall. We stick together two by two and this takes every bit of our attention. We cannot be troubled about others.

Some women fall. The round continues. Schnell. Schnell. The flower bed grows larger. The loop must expand.

Run. Cross over the rickety plank that sags lower and lower—schnell—dump the dirt—schnell—the gate—schnell—refill our aprons—schnell—the gate again—schnell—the plank. It is a delirious race.

For something to think about, we count the blows. At thirty, it is not a bad round. At fifty we stop counting.

The Frenchman is being watched. A kapo is at his side. We can no longer have him give us dirt. Sometimes we exchange glances. Between his teeth, he says: "The bastards, the bastards." A newcomer. Tears come to his eyes. He is sorry for us. It is not so hard for him. He stays in one spot and it is not cold.

Our legs swell. Our features are pinched. With each round we are more exhausted.

Run—schnell—the gate—schnell—the plank—schnell—empty out the dirt—schnell—barbed wire—schnell—the gate—schnell —run—schnell—apron—run—run run run schnell schnell schnell schnell schnell schnell. It is a delirious race.

Each woman watches the others grow uglier and uglier and does not see herself.

A Jewish woman near us leaves the line. She goes up to Taube, talks to him. He opens the gate and gives her a slap that sends her sprawling inside the yard of 25. She has given up. When Taube turns around, he makes a sign to another woman, whom he also flings into the yard of 25. We run as best we can. Do not let him think that we cannot run any longer.

The rounds continue. The sun is high. It is afternoon. The race goes on, the blows and the shrieks. With each round, others fall. Those who have diarrhea smell foul. Streams of diarrhea dry on their legs. We still go round. Just how long will we go round? It is a delirious race run by delirious faces.

As we empty out our aprons, we measure the progress of the bed. We thought that it was finished but the layer of soil was not thick enough. We had to begin again.

The afternoon grows late. The rounds continue. The blows. The shrieks.

When Taube whistled, when the furies shouted: "To the block," we returned supporting one another. Sitting down on our tiers we did not have the strength to take our shoes off. We did not have the strength to talk. We wondered how we had managed again this time.

The next day several of our group went into the sick bay. They went out on the stretcher.

The sky was blue, the sun was out again. It was a Sunday in March.

THE MEN They are waiting in front of the barracks. Silent. In their eyes there is a struggle between resignation and revolt. Resignation has to win.

An SS is guarding them. He shoves them around. Without any apparent reason he suddenly charges them, shouts and strikes. The men remain silent, straighten out their ranks, hold their hands at their sides. They pay no attention to the SS, nor to one another. Each is alone in himself.

Among them there are boys, quite young boys, who do not understand. They watch the men and imitate their grave bearing.

Before going into the barracks, they take their clothes off, fold them, hold them over their arms. They work stripped since the weather has gotten warmer. Undressed they seem to have long white drawers that cling to their bones.

The wait is long. They wait and they know.

It is a new barracks that has just been fitted out in the infirmary compound. Trucks have delivered enameled and nickel-plated apparatus, a miracle of cleanliness that was hard to believe.

They have made the barracks into a radiology and diathermy unit.

The first time that men are being treated in our camp. The men's camp is farther down. It has an infirmary that is better than ours, they say. Maybe only less frightening. Why send them here? Are they going to give people medical care here now?

The men continue to wait. Silent. A far-away look and no color.

One by one, the first men begin to come out. They put their clothes back on at the threshold. Their eyes avoid those of the others who wait. And when we can see their faces we understand.

How could we describe the distress in their gestures? The humiliation in their eyes?

Women are sterilized by surgery.

And what difference does it make? Since none of them is to return. Since none of us will return.

DIALOGUE "Oh! Sally, did you remember what I asked you?"

Sally is running along the Lagerstrasse. By her clothes, we see that she works in Effekts. This is the detail that goes over, sorts and inventories everything in the Jews' baggage, the baggage that the new arrivals leave on the platform. The women who work in Effekts have everything.

"Yes, sweetie, I remembered it, but there isn't any just now. It's been a week since a convoy came in. We're expecting one tonight. From Hungary. It's about time, we have nothing left. So long. See you tomorrow. I'll have the soap for you."

They have just brought water into the camp.

THE COMMANDANT

Two blond boys, hair like the beard of ripe wheat, legs bare, shirtless. Two little boys. Eleven years old, seven years old. Two brothers. Both blond, blue-eyed, tanned. Their necks darker.

The older boy scolds the little one. The little one is bad-tempered. He mutters and finally says, growling:

"No, no. You always get to do it."

"Sure, I'm bigger than you."

"No. It's not fair. I never get to do it."

Reluctantly, because he must talk him into it, the older boy proposes:

"O.K., listen. We'll play some more the same way and then we'll switch. After that we'll each take turns. Is that all right?"

The little one sniffles, detaches himself unwillingly from the wall he has been leaning against, stubbornly, his eyes squinting in the sun and rejoins his brother, shuffling his feet. The other boy shakes him: "You coming? Shall we play?" and he begins to be the person that he wants to be. At the same time he watches to see if the little boy will join in the game. The little boy holds back. He still does not join in the game. He is waiting until his brother is ready.

The big boy gets ready. He buttons up a jacket, straps on a belt, slips his sword in carefully at his side, then adjusts the cap on his head with both hands. He polishes the peak of his cap gently with his cuff, pulls the visor down over his eyes.

As he dresses for the part, his features become stern, and his mouth. His lips grow thin. He throws back his head, as though his eyes were hampered by the visor, arches his waist, puts his left hand behind his back, palm outward; he adjusts an imaginary monocle with the right hand and stares about him.

But now he looks upset. He notices that he has forgotten something. He steps out of character for an instant to get his swagger stick. It is a real swagger stick, lying on the grass—a flexible switch that he regularly plays with—reassumes his pose and taps lightly with the stick on his boots. He is ready. He turns around.

Instantly the little boy steps into character too. He takes less trouble about it. He snaps to attention at the first glance from his brother and immediately takes one step forward, freezes, clicks his heels—the click is not audible, he is barefoot—raises his right arm, stares directly at him with a blank expression. The other responds with a brief salute, just the indication of one, with a superior air. The little boy lowers his arm, clicks his heels again and the big boy starts the march. Erect, his chin tucked in, mouth haughty, the stick swings slightly between his thumb and his forefinger so as to tap against his bare calves. The little boy follows at a distance. He marches less stiffly. A private.

They cross the garden. It is a garden with square lawns and rows of flowers along the edges of the lawns. They cross the garden. The commandant stares the way one conducts inspection, haughtily. The orderly follows and sees nothing, impassive. A soldier.

At the rear of the garden, near a hedge of rose bushes, they halt. The commandant in front, the orderly two steps behind. The commandant takes his place, his right leg thrust a bit forward with the knee a little bent, one hand behind his back, the other holding the swagger stick by the middle on his hip. He holds it over the rose bushes. His expression becomes ugly and he barks out orders. He shouts: "Schnell! Rechts! Links!" His chest swells. "Rechts! Links!" Then he switches: "Links! Rechts!"—faster and faster, louder and louder. "Links! Rechts! Links! Rechts! Links!"—faster, ever faster.

Soon the prisoners to whom these orders are addressed can no longer follow. They stumble on the ground, lose their footing. The commandant is pale with rage. With his switch he strikes, strikes, strikes. Without budging, his shoulders still squared, eyebrows raised. He screams in rage: "Schnell! Schneller! Aber los!" Striking with each order.

Suddenly at the end of the column something is amiss. With a menacing stride he bounds over to his brother who immediately abandons the role of orderly. He now plays the guilty prisoner, his back bent, legs that no longer try to support his body, distraught face, pained mouth, the mouth of someone who can do no more. The commandant takes the swagger stick in the other hand, makes a fist of his right hand, punches him on the chest—a fake punch, he's just playing. The little boy staggers, spins around, and falls flat on the grass. The commandant looks at the prisoner that he has knocked to the ground with contempt, saliva on his lips. And his fury subsides. He feels only disgust. He kicks him— a fake kick, he is barefoot and he's just playing. But the little boy knows the game. The kick turns him over like a limp bag. He lies there, mouth open, eyes glazed over.

Then the big boy, with a sign of the stick to the invisible prisoners that surround him, commands: "Zum Krematorium," and moves on. Stiff, satisfied and disgusted.

The commandant of the camp lives quite close by, beyond the electrified barbed-wire fence. A brick house, with a rose garden and lawn, brilliantly colored begonias in blue flower boxes. Between the rose hedge and the barbed-wire fence is the path that leads to the crematory oven. This is the path the stretchers follow carrying the dead. The dead go by one after another all day long. The chimney smokes all day long. The passing hours shift the shadow of the chimney over the sandy walks and over the lawns.

The commandant's sons play in the garden. They play horses, balloon, or else they play commandant and prisoner.

"Naturally, my family wanted for nothing. The least desire of my wife and children was satisfied without delay. The children could run about freely. My wife took care of her little 'floral paradise'"

—Rudolf Hœss in *Commandant of Auschwitz*

ROLL CALL It is interminable this morning.

The blockhovas fuss, count, re-count. The SS in cloaks go from one group to another, go to the office, come out with papers that they check. They check the figures of this human accounting. Roll call will last until the figures come out right.

Taube arrives. He takes charge of the search. With his dog he goes off to rummage through the blocks. The blockhovas get edgy, punch and lash out in every direction. Each hopes that it is not her block that is short.

We wait.

The SS in cloaks look over the figures, check the human sums once more.

We wait.

Taube returns. He has found something. He whistles softly to urge the dog following him on. The dog is dragging a woman by the nape of the neck.

Taube leads his dog to the block detail that the woman belonged to. The count comes out right.

Taube gives a blast on the whistle. Roll call is finished.

Someone says: "Let's hope she was dead."

LULU We had been at the bottom of this ditch since morning. There were three of us. The detail was working farther on. The kapos merely prodded us from time to time to see how far we had gotten with the ditch we were digging. We could talk. We had been talking since morning.

Talking was making plans for our return because believing in our return was a way of forcing luck. The women who had stopped believing in their return were dead. We had to believe, to believe despite everything, against all odds, to make this return convincing, to give it reality and color, while we prepared for it, while we conjured it up in all its details.

Sometimes a woman, giving voice to all our thoughts, interrupted with: "But can you see us getting out?" We came to. The question died away in silence.

In order to shake off this silence and the anxiety that it masked, another woman ventured: "Perhaps one day we will not be awakened for roll call. We will sleep late. When we wake up it will be broad daylight. The camp will be all quiet. The women who go out of the barracks first will notice that the guard post is empty, that the towers are empty. All the SS will have fled. A few hours later the first Russian advance units will be here."

Another silence answered this anticipation.

She added: "Earlier we will have heard artillery fire. Far away at first, then closer and closer. The battle of Krakow. When Krakow falls it will be over. You'll see, the SS will run away."

The more details she gave, the less we believed. By tacit agreement we dropped the subject in order to get back to our plans, those unrealizable plans that had the logic of madmen's conversations.

We had been talking since morning. We were glad to be separated from the gang because we did not hear the screams of the kapos. We did not receive the blows that punctuate the screams. The ditch grew deeper as the hours passed. Our heads no longer came over the top. When we reached a layer of limestone our feet were in water. The mud that we threw over our heads was white. It was not cold—one of the first days that it was no longer cold. The sun warmed our shoulders. We were at peace.

An SS comes along. She shouts. She makes my two companions climb out and leads them off. The ditch is almost deep enough, three are not needed to finish it. They go off and say good-by to me reluctantly. They know the fear that every woman has of being separated from the others, of being alone. To cheer me, they say: "Hurry up, you'll be back with us."

I remain alone at the bottom of this ditch and I am overcome with despair. The presence of the others, their words, made return possible. They went away and I am afraid. I do not believe in the return when I am alone. With them, since they seem to believe in it so firmly, I believe in it too. The minute they leave me, I am afraid. No one believes in the return when she is alone.

Here I am at the bottom of this ditch, alone, so discouraged that I wonder if I will get to the end of the day. How many hours to go before the blast of the whistle signals the end of work, the moment when we re-form the column to go back to camp, in ranks of five, giving our arms to one another, and talking, talking to distraction?

I am alone here. I can no longer think of anything because all my thoughts collide with the anxiety that grips all of us: How shall we get out of here? When shall we get out of here? I would like to think of nothing. And if that continues no one will get out. The women who are still alive tell themselves every day that it is a miracle to have held out for eight weeks. No one can see more than a week ahead of herself.

I am alone and I am afraid. I try to get engrossed in digging. The work does not progress. I attack a last bump to even out the bottom, perhaps the kapo will decide that that is enough. My back feels bruised, paralyzed from bending over, my shoulders feel wrenched out of their sockets by the shovel, my arms no longer have the strength to toss the shovelfuls of muddy chalk over the edge. I am here alone. I want to lie down in the mud and wait. Wait for the kapo to find me dead. Not so easy to die. One must beat people with a shovel or a club for a very long time before they die.

I dig a bit more. I scoop out two or three shovelfuls more. This is too hard. As soon as one is alone one thinks: What's the use? Why do it? Why not give up? . . . Just as well now. With others, one keeps going.

I am alone, hurrying to finish so that I can rejoin my comrades and tempted to give up. Why? Why should I dig this ditch?

"Enough. That's enough." A voice above me shrieks: "Komm, schnell!" I use the shovel to help myself climb out. How weary my arms are, how painful the back of my neck is. The kapo is running. I must follow her. She crosses the road to the edge of the marsh. The fill project. Women like ants. Some carry sand to others who level the ground with pounders. A big flat space full of sun. Hundreds of women standing, in a frieze of shadows against the sunlight.

I arrive behind the kapo who hands me at the same time both a pounder and a scraper and sends me toward a group. I look around for my friends. Lulu calls me: "Come over here, there's room," and she moves a bit to one side so that

I can be next to her in the line of women beating the ground, holding the pounder that they raise and drop with both hands. "Come here pasty-face!" How can Viva find the strength to yell that? I cannot move my lips even to suggest a smile. Lulu is worried: "What's the matter with you? Are you sick?"

"No, I'm not sick. I can't take it any more. Today I just can't take it any more."

"It's nothing. You'll get over it."

"No, Lulu, I won't get over it. I tell you I can't take any more."

She has no answer to give. It is the first time she has heard me talk this way. A practical woman, she hefts my implement. "How heavy your pounder is. Take mine. It's lighter and you're more tired than I am from that ditch."

We exchange implements. I begin to pound the sand too. I watch all these women making the same gestures with their arms weaker and weaker from lifting the heavy weight, the kapos with their clubs going from one woman to another, and despair overwhelms me. "How shall we ever get out of here?"

Lulu looks at me. She smiles at me. Her hand brushes mine to comfort me. And I repeat to make her realize that it is useless: "I tell you that today I really can't take it any more. This time I mean it."

Lulu looks around us, sees that no kapo is near for the moment, grabs me by the wrist and says: "Get behind me. so they don't see you. You can have a good cry." She speaks softly, timidly. No doubt this is just what I need since I obey her gentle shove. I drop my implement, I stand there leaning on the handle and I cry. I did not want to cry, but the tears spill over, run down my cheeks. I let them run down and when a tear touches my lips, I taste its saltiness and I go on crying.

Lulu works and keeps watch. Sometimes she turns around and with her sleeve, she gently wipes my face. I cry. I think of nothing, I cry.

I no longer know why I am crying when Lulu tugs at me: "That's all now. Come work. There she is."

With so much kindness that I am not ashamed of having cried. It is as though I had cried on my mother's breast.

THE ORCHESTRA

It stood on an embankment near the gate.

The woman who was conducting had been famous in Vienna. All the women were good musicians. They had taken a test in order to be selected from among a great number. They owed their reprieve to music.

Because in the warmer months an orchestra had been necessary. At least in so far as the new commandant was concerned. He loved music. When he ordered them to play for him, he had an extra half loaf of bread passed out to the musicians. And when the new arrivals alighted from the boxcars to go in ranks to the gas chamber, he liked it to be to the rhythm of a gay march.

They played in the mornings when the columns started out. As we passed we had to keep time. Later they played waltzes. Waltzes that we had heard elsewhere in an obliterated past. Hearing them here was unbearable.

Seated on stools, they play. Do not look at the fingers of the cellist, nor at her eyes when she plays, you will not be able to bear it.

Do not look at the gestures of the woman who is conducting. She parodies the woman that she was in the large café in Vienna where she once conducted a female orchestra, and it is obvious that she is thinking of what she used to be.

All of them are wearing navy blue pleated skirts, light blouses, lavender kerchiefs over their heads. They are dressed this way in order to set the pace for the others who go to the marshes in the dresses they sleep in, otherwise the dresses would never dry out.

The columns have gone. The orchestra stays a moment longer.

Do not look, do not listen, especially if they play the

119

"Merry Widow" while beyond the second barbed-wire fence men emerge one after another from the barracks and the kapos strike them one after another with belts as they emerge, naked.

Do not look at the orchestra playing the "Merry Widow."

Do not listen. You would only hear the blows on the men's backs and the metallic clicks that the buckles make when the belts fly.

Do not look at the musicians who play while skeleton-like naked men come out under blows that make them stagger. They are going to delousing because there are definitely too many lice in that barracks.

Do not look at the violinist. She is playing on a violin that would be Yehudi's if Yehudi were not miles and miles away across the ocean. What Yehudi did this violin belong to?

Do not look, do not listen.

Do not think of all the Yehudis who had brought their violins.

SO YOU BELIEVED So you believed that only
solemn words rose to the lips of the dying
    because solemnity naturally flourishes at the deathbed
    a bed is always ready for the pomp of a funeral
    with the family at the bedside
    sincere sorrow the prevailing mood.

Naked on the foul beds of the sick bay nearly all our
comrades have said:
"This time I'm going to croak."
They were naked on the bare boards.
They were dirty and the boards were foul with diarrhea
and pus.
They did not realize that they were complicating the job of
those who would survive who would have to report their
last words to their relatives. Their relatives expected something solemn. Impossible to disappoint them. The trivial has
no place in the anthology of deathbed pronouncements.
But one does not permit oneself to be weak.
Therefore they said "I'm going to croak" so as not to
undermine the courage of the others
    and they counted so little on a single survival that they
confided nothing that could be construed as a message.

SPRINGTIME All these lumps of flesh which had lost the pinkness and the life of flesh were strewn about in the dusty dried mud, were completing the process of withering and decomposing in the sunlight. All this brownish, purplish, gray flesh blended in so well with the dusty soil that it required an effort to pick out the women there, to make out empty breasts amid this puckered skin that hung from women's chests.

O you who said farewell to them on the threshold of a prison or on the threshold of your death on a morning tarnished by long vigils, happy are you who cannot see what they have done to your women, to their breasts that you had dared touch one last time on the threshold of death, women's breasts ever so soft, a softness so overwhelming to you who were about to die—your wives.

It required an effort to make out faces in the features where pupils no longer shone, faces that were the color of ashes or dirt, hewn out of rotting stumps or broken off a very old bas-relief although time had not succeeded in wearing down the cheek bones—a jumble of heads—heads without hair, incredibly tiny—owl heads with disproportionate brow ridges —all these sightless faces—heads and faces, body against body half-reclining in the mud that had dried to dust.

Amid the rags—next to these what you call rags would be drapery—amid the dirt-stained tatters hands appeared—hands appeared because they moved, because fingers bent and contracted, because they rummaged amid the rags, poked into armpits, and lice crunched between thumb nails. Blood made brown spots on the nails that squashed the lice.

What remained of life in their eyes and in their hands lived on in this gesture—but their legs in the dust—bare legs oozing with sores, gouged with wounds—their legs in the dust were inert like wooden legs—inert—heavy their heads bent forward hung on their necks like wooden heads—heavy

and the women who in the warmth of the first bit of sunlight were stripping off their rags to delouse them, uncovering their necks that were now only knots and cords, their shoulders that were just collar bones, their chests on which the breasts did not prevent one from seeing the rib-hoops

all these women leaning against one another, motionless in the mud dried to dust, rehearsed without realizing

—they realized, you know—that is still more terrible

rehearsed the scene in which they would die the next day— or one day very soon

for each woman dies her death a thousand times.

The next day or one day very soon, they would be corpses in the dust that replaced the snow and mud of winter. They had held on all winter—in the marshes, in the mud, in the snow. They could not get past the first warm sunny day.

The first warm sunshine of the year on the bare earth.

The earth for the first time was not a hostile element, threatening every step—if you fall, if you let yourself fall you will not get up—

For the first time we could sit down on the ground.

The earth, bare for the first time, dry for the first time, ceased to cast its dizzying spell, its invitation to let oneself slip to the ground—to let oneself slip into death as though into snow—into oblivion—to give up—to stop giving orders to one's arms, to one's legs and to so many lesser muscles so that none would let go, in order to keep on one's feet—in order to stay alive—to slip—to let oneself slip into the snow— to let oneself slip into death with its soft snowy embrace.

The thick mud and the filthy snow were for the first time dust.

Dry dust, warmed by the sun

it is harder to die in the dust

harder to die when the sun is shining.

The sun shone—pale as in the east. The sky was very blue. Somewhere spring was singing.

Spring sang in my memory—in my memory.

This song surprised me so much that I was not sure that I heard it. I thought I was hearing it in a dream. And I tried to deny it, not to hear it and I cast a despairing glance at my companions around me. They were clustered there in the sun, in the space that separated the barracks from the barbed-wire fences. The barbed wire was so white in the sun.

That Sunday.

An extraordinary Sunday because it was a rest Sunday and we were permitted to sit on the ground.

All of the women were seated in the dust of the dried mud in a pitiable swarm that made one think of flies on a dung hill. No doubt because of the smell. The smell was so strong and so fetid that we thought that we were breathing not air but some thicker and more viscous fluid that enveloped and shut off this part of the world with an additional atmosphere in which only specially adapted creatures could move. Us.

A stench of diarrhea and of carrion. Above this stench the sky was blue. And in my memory spring was singing.

Why had I alone of all these beings kept my memory? In my memory spring was singing. Why this difference?

Silvery pussywillows sparkled in the sun—a poplar bends in the wind—the grass is so green that the spring flowers shimmer with surprising colors. Spring bathes everything in a light, light intoxicating air. Spring goes to one's head. Spring is a symphony bursting forth on every side, bursting, bursting.

Bursting. In my bursting head.

Why have I kept my memory? Why this injustice?

And from my memory emerge only such poor images that tears of despair overtake me.

In the spring, walking along the embankments, and the plane trees of the Louvre are such fine tracery next to the chestnuts of the Tuileries which are already in full leaf.

In the spring going through the Luxembourg Gardens before work at the office. Children running on the paths, bookbags under their arms. Children. To think of children here.

In the spring the blackbird in the acacia tree beneath the window wakes before daybreak. Even before daybreak it had been learning to whistle. It still whistles poorly. It is only the beginning of April.

Why leave me only my memory? And my memory finds only clichés. "My beautiful ship, O my memory . . ." Where are you, my true memory? Where are you, my earthly memory?

The sky was very blue a blue so blue on the white cement posts and on the white barbed wire too, a blue so blue that the network of electric lines seemed whiter, more implacable,

here nothing is green

here nothing is growing

here nothing is alive.

Far beyond the wires spring hovers, spring thrills, spring sings. In my memory. Why have I kept my memory?

Why keep the memory of streets with echoing pavements, of the fifes of spring on the benches of the fruit sellers at the market, shafts of sunlight on the light parquet floor when I got up, the remembrance of laughter and of hats, bells in the evening air, of the first blouses and of anemones.

Here the sun is not the spring sun. It is the sun of eternity, it is the sun before creation. And I had kept the memory of the sun that shines on the world of the living, of the sun on the world of wheat.

Under the sun of eternity, flesh ceases to throb, eyelids turn blue, hands wither, tongues swell black, mouths rot.

Here outside of time, under the sun before creation, eyes grow pale. Eyes dim. Lips grow pale. Lips die.

All words have wilted long ago

All words have faded long ago

Grass—umbels—spring—brook—lilacs—spring showers—all the images have long been pale.

Why have I kept my memory? I cannot rediscover the taste of my saliva in my mouth in the spring—the taste of a sprig of grass that one sucks. I cannot rediscover the smell of hair in which the wind plays, his reassuring hand and his tenderness.

My memory is more bloodless than an autumn leaf

My memory has forgotten dew

My memory has lost its sap. My memory has lost all its blood.

It is then that the heart should stop beating—stop beating —beating.

This is the reason why I cannot go over to the woman who is calling me. My neighbor. Is she calling? Why is she calling? All of a sudden she has death on her face, violet death at the sides of her nostrils, death deep in her eye sockets, death in her fingers that twist and crumple like twigs that a flame devours, and she speaks in an unknown tongue words which I do not hear.

The barbed wire is very white against the blue sky.

Was she calling me? She is still now, her head slumped in the befouled dust.

Far beyond the barbed wire spring is singing.

Her eyes have emptied out

And we have lost our memory.

None of us will return.

126

None of us should have returned

Charlotte Delbo joined the Resistance movement at the very beginning of the Nazi occupation in France, together with her husband, Georges Dudach. Both were arrested in Paris on March 2, 1942, by the French police and handed over to the Gestapo. Dudach was shot on May 23, 1942, at Mont-Valérien. Charlotte Delbo was first imprisoned in La Santé and Fort de Romainville and was deported to Auschwitz in January, 1943.

Today she says: "I am no longer sure that what I have written is true, but I am sure that it happened."